COSMIC BIBLE

Paradigm Revolution
by Paradoxical Truth

BOOK 4

Minoru Uba

Copyright © 2015 by Minoru Uba

COSMIC BIBLE BOOK 4

Published by Babel Press U.S.A.
All rights reserved.
Date of publication: August 20, 2015

This book was originally published in Japanese under the title "宇宙聖書" by VOICE, Japan in 2010.

Author: Minoru Uba

Director: Tomoki Hotta

Original translation by Self-Healing Study and Practice Group
Edited and translated by Gyoko Koike

Coordinator: Junko Rodriguez
Formatting: Sota Torigoe

ISBN: 978-0989232654

Babel Corporation
Pacific Business News Bldg. #208,
1833 Kalakaua Avenue,
Honolulu, Hawaii 96815

Phone: (808) 946 - 3773
Fax: (808) 946 - 3993

Website: http://www.bookandright.com/

CONTENTS

Chapter Four☆The Conclusion

4-1. Definition of truth and fact in the PARAREVO theory……11
4-2. There is no fact better than truth……12
4-3. Internal nature of truth and external nature of fact……15
4-4. External separation of fact and internal separation of truth……18
4-5. Self-integration of truth and Self-domination of fact……20
4-6. "Thought of remorse" of truth and "thought of grudge" of fact ……22
4-7. Verification of the way of life of Jesus and the way of life of PARAREVO……26
4-8. Logos for the way of life of PARAREVO……32
4-9. Truth is in now and fact is in time axis……33
4-10. Life is with Self-determination and Self-responsibility……36
4-11. Universe is undeniable existentialism……38
4-12. Truth, the innermost secret to live in the "Now"……40
4-13. The rule of "spirit is subjective and body is objective" will release the genetic linkage……42
4-14. The PARAREVO theory shows the "rule of the attainment of the spiritual being during life"……44
4-15. The "rule of genetic linkage" will lead to unhealthy dependence and shift responsibility to others……48
4-16. Self-integration in the thought of child and parents……50
4-17. The now will release causality under the time axis……52
4-18. Life is based on the rule of Self-responsibility……53
4-19. Addiction to religion is similar to schizophrenia……54
4-20. Flashback phenomena of consciousness of past lives……58
4-21. Emerging consciousness is the final chapter of spiritual evolution……61
4-22. View of life in the universe and on the earth is paradoxical theory and rule……65
4-23. The mechanism of birth of lives born on the earth……67
4-24. The Relative relationship between the physical body and the soul……68

4-25. The rule of causality and the rule of karma will collapse 71
4-26. Spiritual evolution and the "exclusion theory by jealousy" are opposite......74
4-27. Logos to release emerging consciousness......77
4-28. Logos to live in the "Now"......78
4-29. Separation of "I" is the true way of life......79
4-30. Separation borderline between love and kindness......83
4-31. Only truth exists in the spiritual world......85
4-32. Lose truth being fooled by fact......88
4-33. Separation borderline between self and others in the personality formation history......90
4-34. Time to face the natural world seriously......91
4-35. The time for judgment by water......93
4-36. Now is the time to receive judgment from water......94
4-37. Separation borderlines between oneself and others in the material world......97
4-38. The natural environment and truth of separation borderline between oneself and others......99
4-39. The personality formation history based on the social environment and the view of values......103
4-40. Outer evaluation as fact and inner evaluation as truth......104
4-41. The foundation of the Constitution is established by religions 109
4-42. The 20th century was the era of ideological strife......112
4-43. The 21st century is the era of religious strife......113
4-44. The 21st century is the era to release from religious spell 115
4-45. Religion exists in our individual truth......117
4-46. Religious dependence and shifting responsibility by victim consciousness......118
4-47. Religious dependence and chain of unhappiness......121
4-48. The vertical and horizontal personality formation history 123
4-49. Prenatal environment and the ground environment of saints are paradox......124
4-50. Habit of mind is inherited from mother......126

4-51. Roles and responsibilities of a couple with ideal love......129
4-52. Material wealth produces poor mind......130
4-53. Separation borderline between self and others and true spiritual relationship of parent-child......132
4-54. Marital relationship is the second ONSHU......133
4-55. Love pair system and the relative original power......135
4-56. The 4 rules of relativity based on the spiritual dimension 141
4-57. The historical perspective of legalized male dominating structure......143
4-58. Love of women and men is the height of "the relative art" 146
4-59. The time axis is like a virtual world......151
4-60. Evolution is the way to release from the time axis domination 155
4-61. Women who are in the high-spiritual dimension are the driving force of evolution......157
4-62. The way of life of PARAREVO transcends the time-axis 160
4-63. Spiritual consciousness and physical consciousness are paradox......162
4-64. The principal of dimensional integration of the cosmological love......163
4-65. Establish Self-integrity by the way of PARAREVO life......166
4-66. SHINSEI is the receptor for everything in the universe......171
4-67. SHINSEI is the receptor for everything of the entire personality......172
4-68. The importance of Logos and the concept of way of life......174
4-69. All things necessary have to be good......178
4-70. True Self-realization is unconditional Self-completion......180
4-71. The way of PARAREVO life makes your entire life "truly lucky"......183
4-72. The rule of freedom is the fundamental rule of the universe 185
4-73. SHINSEI itself evolves by the rule of freedom......187
4-74. The 21st century is the end of monotheism......189
4-75. The rule of freedom based on Self-responsibility......190

4-76. The rule of the relative field based on love......193
4-77. Individual mental entities manifest individual art......195
4-78. Individual subjectivity makes individual art sustainable......198
4-79. Individual subjectivity releases the past practice of causality 200
4-80. Individual subjectivity builds global collaboration......201
4-81. Individual subjectivity leads historical evolution......203
4-82. Individuality integrates subject of love and object of happiness 205
4-83. The principle of integration of love and the principle of domination of ONSHU......206
4-84. The earth star is the planet of legalized domination structure 208
4-85. The dominating structure of the brain is the center of physical domination......209
4-86. The physical dominating structure is the root of all evil in the rule of reincarnation......212
4-87. The dominating structure on the earth star is the unique structure of the universe......213
4-88. Manifestation of SHINSEI integration consciousness world by PARAREVO......214
4-89. The true view of life and death based on the rule of the attainment of the spiritual being during life......216
4-90. The 21st century is the watershed in human history......218
4-91. How do we resolve discrimination in the world?......220
4-92. How do we resolve the gap between rich and poor?......222
4-93. How do we resolve the disparity in civilization?......223
4-94. How do we resolve the religious conflicts?......225
4-95. Free from the boundaries between race and nations......227
4-96. Equation for releasing core of ONSHU......230
4-97. Transition to female supremacy from male supremacy......235
4-98. The way for solving problems on the earth......237
4-99. Challenge "the era of termination" in religions......240
4-100. The PARAREVO theory is the thought of remorse......245
4-101. Homo-cosmology and "Regeneration of SHINSEI and soul" 250

Chapter 4

Conclusion

Chapter Four ☆ The Conclusion

4-1. Definition of truth and fact in the PARAREVO theory

The PARAREVO theory distinguishes and defines clearly, the difference between truth and fact, which is, truth is defined as *the existence of the consciousness based on SHINSEI*, and fact is defined as *the existence of the phenomenon based on things*. Since *truth is the existence of the consciousness based on SHINSEI, it exists in the consciousness of the person, and doesn't matter whether it evokes "soul mind" or "body mind." Truth is nothing but truth, and is not affected by the theory of good or bad, and superiority or inferiority, and fact is the existence of the phenomenon based on things, so all matters and physical phenomena, including the body, are happening outside the consciousness.*

Included in the definitions of truth and fact, are the rule of the universe and the rule of the earth, as totally opposite theories. I will now distinguish and define the fundamental difference of truth and fact according to the PARAREVO theory. Truth is defined based on the rule of "spirit is subjective and body is objective," and fact is defined based on the rule of "body is subjective and spirit is objective." Therefore, the definition of truth and fact, used as a general concept, are totally opposite.

In the PARAREVO theory, the theoretical frameworks and values have totally opposite definitions. For example, truth of zero time and fact of the time axis, truth of internal nature and fact of external nature, truth of internal separation and fact of external separation, truth of the principle of dimensional integration and fact of the principle of dimensional domination, truth of Self-integration and fact of Self-domination, truth of the principle of

Chapter Four ☆ The Conclusion

Self-responsibility and fact of the principle of shifting responsibility, truth of wrongdoer consciousness and fact of victim consciousness, and truth of the ideology of remorse and fact of the ideology of grudge.

People who live the way of life of PARAREVO try to draw a separation boundary between themselves and others to make clear the difference between *the existence of the consciousness based on SHINSEI* as the cause of subjectivity and *the existence of the phenomenon based on things* as the result of objectivity, and direct themselves to a higher spiritual dimension as the relative subjectivity.

I would like to verify the contrary nature, in detail, of the way of life of truth by the cosmological evidence, based on the PARAREVO theory, and the way of life of fact by the earth logical evidence, and show the essence of the way of life of PARAREVO.

4-2. There is no fact better than truth

Since truth connotes in your consciousness based on your own spiritual dimension, all other things are considered as fact. For example, suppose you are imprisoned by false charges because people around you believed you committed the crime, when in fact, your neighbor did. In verifying the chain of events, the crime happened as the physical phenomenon no matter whether you did it or not. That is the fact for you. Now, if you make your consciousness cruel and are a violent person who holds grudges, and curses, and go into a rage because of the fact that you were imprisoned by false charges even though you were innocent, this consciousness itself would become your truth.

On the other hand, whether it is a false charge or judgment of innocent offense, the fact that happened is the fact by which your inner cause, problem and assignment become phenomenon, so you should accept as it is unconditionally and totally with gratitude and happiness by directing the arrow to yourself and understand deeply and repent, then the existence of the consciousness of yourself is the truth for you. Truth exists in your spirit and mind as your Self-determination of the consciousness, all other things are merely phenomena and only fact.

Directing truth is to shoulder Self-responsibility with Self-determination for the choice of the consciousness based on the rule of freedom, whether you evoke love of the "soul mind" with SHINSEI as the basis and *accept the fact unconditionally and totally with gratitude and happiness,* or whether you evoke hatred of the "body mind" with SHINSEI as the basis and *fall into unpleasant feelings with deep-seated hatred and hard feelings by shifting responsibility to the phenomenon, and also have the victim consciousness by being at the mercy of the fact* and reach to Self-destruction by Self-injurious behavior. This is the real truth as the existence of the consciousness based on SHINSEI, and the way of the PARAREVO theory based on the rule of the universe.

The definition of truth is *the existence of the exercised consciousness with SHINSEI as the basis, no matter whether it is the "soul mind" or the "body mind," or good or bad.* It is because the fact of the theory of good and bad, or superiority or inferiority in this world does not have any meaning or significance in the spiritual world. Only truth is asked in the spiritual world, and

Chapter Four ☆ The Conclusion

fact in this world, if you are guilty or not-guilty, innocent or falsely charged, does not matter. How you evoke the consciousness based on SHINSEI toward the fact is asked of yourself.

If you fall into the poor and ugly mind and spirit like a cruel and violent person, exhausting all kinds of ONSHU, cursing people, holding grudges and hard feelings, you have no choice but to go to the spiritual world like an ugly, cruel, and violent person. However, if you accept any kind of fact as it is with gratitude and happiness, you will go to the spiritual world, fulfilled with gratitude and happiness.

For example, cancer is only the fact of the physical phenomenon, and if your consciousness is dominated by the fact and you fall into uncomfortable feelings such as insecurity and fear, illness exists as truth, because you are taken ill in your mind. In fact, illness is written with two Japanese Kanji characters as distressing the mind. If you consider cancer merely as the fact of the physical phenomenon and accept it with gratitude and happiness, the truth, called illness, does not exist because you are not distressing the mind.

Since there is no fact better than truth, truth certainly surpasses fact and transcends it, and it will be able to overcome the cancer. Therefore, fact as the Self-centered cancer is surpassed by truth as love, and will be overcome and disappear. If the truth of the soul is dominated by the fact of the body, based on the rule of "body is subjective and spirit is objective," you will reach to Self-destruction by the expansion of disharmony and disorder. If the truth of the soul could integrate the fact of the body, based on the rule of "spirit is subjective and body is objective," the cancer cell itself selects apoptosis and reaches Self-destruction.

People who live the way of PARAREVO always try to live with the truth rather than with the fact, and make the best effort to overcome and change the bad habit of mind. This is because they understand that there is no fact better than truth.

4-3. Internal nature of truth and external nature of fact

The PARAREVO theory suggests establishing Self-integration by clearly drawing the separation boundary line between oneself and others and distinguishing the internal nature of oneself and the external nature of others. For example, all kinds of matters occurring outside oneself such as all natural phenomena and social phenomena are *the existence of the phenomenon based on things* by the rule of "body is subjective and spirit is objective." This is defined as *the external nature of fact*.

It is totally your own determination to conclude those facts, whether with gratitude and joy by the relative original power between SHINSEI and the "soul mind," or with unpleasant feelings by the relative original power between SHINSEI and the "body mind," based on the rule of "spirit is subjective and body is objective" and the rule of freedom. Either way, you should reach Self-completion by shouldering Self-responsibility with your existence of the consciousness based on SHINSEI. This is called *the internal nature of truth*.

Thus, *truth connotes in the internal consciousness of oneself, and fact is the phenomenon of things existing outside of your*

Chapter Four ☆ The Conclusion

consciousness including the physical body.

For instance, the natural phenomenon such as it is raining, is the common fact equal to everybody. It will be your decision how to acknowledge this natural phenomenon and acknowledge by your "soul mind" with gratitude and happiness, or your "body mind" with unpleasant feelings.

I think the general public and mass media in the non-PARAREVO world acknowledge the fact of the phenomenon called typhoon with unpleasant feelings, and consider it as something terrible and annoying. On the other hand, people who live the life of PARAREVO take the fact called typhoon as truth. They feel the intention and the consciousness of the typhoon and consider it as the best *lucky Feng Shui* (a Chinese philosophical system of harmonizing the human existence with the surrounding environment), which means that wind and water give the great blessing and benefit from nature, and believe it is the "surprising phenomenon" for *purification and regeneration of the nature world*. The intention of wind and water purifies unclean things and pours new vitality. So, they express their happiness and attain their Self-completion as truth of gratitude and joy.

All kinds of phenomena, such as physical phenomenon like illness, and social phenomenon are fact and never reach to truth at all. Those facts exist around us limitlessly. However, truth is directed and completed by a consciousness evoked by the relative wave and the rule of the relative original power between SHINSEI of each person and the personal dimension (the dimension of the mind), and the spirituality dimension (the dimension of the soul).

Those who are in the lower spiritual dimension in the "Astral lower level," dominated by the physical world benefits and poor and self-centered mind are easy to fall into the poor truth, and Self-complete to unpleasant feelings, no matter what the fact is. When it rains, they complain about rain, when sunny days continue they complain and want rain, when it is cold they complain because it is cold, and when it is hot they complain because it is hot. They complain about everything, such as that or this person is bad, the husband or wife is bad, the father-in-law or the mother-in-law is bad, the child is bad, the parents are bad, the school is bad, the company is bad, the society is bad, the politics is bad, the nation is bad, the knees hurts, or the back hurts, etc. and direct the causes of all bad things to the outside of their consciousness, shifting responsibility to other things and making excuses for themselves by falling to victim consciousness. They make the unpleasant feelings by themselves, invite Self-destruction by Self-hatred and do Self-injurious behavior, inflicting a wound on their soul.

Those who live the way of PARAREVO in the higher spiritual entity dimension in the "Causal level" never make a fool of themselves because of the fact. They aim for the way of life to *accept as they are unconditionally and totally with gratitude and happiness* based on truth.

As you can see, when you acknowledge the subjectivity and the cause, whether it is the internal truth based on the rule of "spirit is subjective and body is objective," or whether it is the external fact based on the rule of "body is subjective and spirit is objective," objectivity and the result become totally opposite.

Those who live the way of PARAREVO understand that the existing purpose and value of life is to prepare for the spiritual life, aim to direct to *the compensation of truth* which is the achievement of love built in the spiritual consciousness entity for the spiritual benefit, not to *the compensation of fact* built by the physical world benefits such as status, reputation and property, and clarify the concept of the way of life without lies, untruth and deception.

It is because *there is no fact better than truth* in the spiritual world.

4-4. External separation of fact and internal separation of truth

In order for us to live in the higher spiritual dimension with truth, we must understand that all existing things inevitably contain opposite matters by the rule of entropy relativity. There is no theory of good or bad, and superiority or inferiority. We must accept as it is by learning the acceptance degree of love and the freedom degree of consciousness, unconditionally and totally.

In our consciousnesses, there are two directly opposite natures existing. One is the consciousness directed to outside and the other is the consciousness directed to inside.

The non-PAREVO way of life is to always direct your eyes to the outside and make the external separation by external evaluation based on the rule of "body is subjective and spirit is objective," and by continuing to strengthen fierce and evil competition by the academic supremacy principle, the economic supremacy principle and the merit-based principle. According to this dimensional domination, we are directed to Self-injurious behavior by falling into Self-hatred and end up heading to Self-destruction. We have a tendency to neglect truth, because we have the habit of evoking our consciousness by external evaluation by using only our physical eyes, and being at the mercy of fact. Court trials are performed based on the theory of good or bad, so it is deliberated based on the physical evidence. The internal evaluation is not as important as the physical evidence. In our class ranking society, the evaluation of a person is by academic background and high status, but not so much by internal evaluation. The material and art worlds are also evaluated by the authorized persons or economic reasons, but not so much by internal evaluation.

In the way of life of PARAREVO, the eyes of the spiritual consciousness entity always direct to inside and make internal separation by internal evaluation based on the rule of "spirit is subjective and body is objective," so the "soul mind," which is the intention of the relative subjectivity, surpasses the "body mind," which is the intention of the relative objectivity, and continues to expand the creation of joy according to the good motivation based on love, and they direct to Self-affection and achieve Self-creation.

Since truth is the existence of the consciousness based on SHINSEI, the intention of the relative subjectivity (the spiritual consciousness entity) and the relative objectivity (the desire of the body) always struggle with each other in the slight fluctuation of imperfection, and is led to Self-determination, Self-responsibility and Self-completion, based on the rule of freedom of each person. Therefore, we should not make evaluation of others and criticize or gossip about others with external separation by external evaluation. Instead, we should make Self-effort to raise the internal evaluation of ourselves, by internal separation of the "soul mind" and the "body mind" inside ourselves, according to the principle of dimensional integration.

Those who live the way of PARAREVO aim not to be deceived by *the reward of fact* without any guarantee, but aim to live for *the reward of truth* which guarantees the eternal life.

4-5. Self-integration of truth and Self-domination of fact

People who live the way of PARAREVO face the objectivity and the result of fact seriously and verify it with the PARAREVO theory, humbly. They try to dismiss and surpass the domination nature of the "body mind" by the integrity nature of the "soul mind," and direct to a higher spiritual dimension and achieve Self-Enlightenment and spiritual evolution, in order to complete the responsibility of assignment with the subjectivity and the cause of their own truth. They understand that all phenomena that happen as fact are the shadow of truth based on their own spiritual dimension because truth of each person is based on the spiritual dimension of each person.

The same fact is totally different in the way it is acknowledged between the lower human beings in the "Astral lower level dimension," who are dominated by undifferentiated sexual desire consciousness, and the higher human beings in the "Causal higher level dimension," who are under the highly differentiated sexual integration consciousness, and truth is directed to the totally opposite consciousness.

For example, even though you haven`t done anything but are

treated as a criminal or discriminated against by other people's supposition or wrong impression, this is fact. However, those who live the way of PARAREVO understand that the reason the fact was drawn out from the cause, the problem, and the assignment, connoted by themselves, so they try to manage the fact based on their own internal nature, and verify it based on the PARAREVO theory, and complete the truth in directing to the higher spiritual dimension, by drawing the separation boundary line between themselves and the primary factor of this fact based on the external nature.

Whether you acknowledge these phenomena by the "soul mind," which is the relative subjectivity inside yourself, or whether you acknowledge them by the "body mind," which is the relative objectivity, is the truth in the spiritual dimension of each person. I call the former acknowledgement *the dimensional integration of truth* and the latter is *the dimensional domination of truth*.

For example, people who always have unpleasant feelings inside as the subjectivity and cause of truth, such as complaints, jealousy, abusive action, anger, anxiety and fear, will embody unpleasant situations as the objectivity and result of fact, and things which cause unpleasant feelings occur as the phenomenon. People who live with delusions and illusions such as speculation and conjecture of the general public, or those who are made fools of by facts are always dominated by unpleasant feelings with excuses and shifting responsibility, and falling into victim consciousness.

People who live the way of PARAREVO, make every effort to avoid measuring truth with speculation and conjecture toward the objective fact by rumors or mass media, and manage fact as much as possible. And they try to reach the result by directing to truth.

In order to guarantee the rule of freedom, we must be secure by ourselves and direct to Self-management by Self-determination and Self-completion by Self-responsibility. The universe imposes strict principles in order to guarantee freedom. It is because it follows the fundamental principle that *freedom is guaranteed with security, called responsibility.* Freedom without responsibility is equal to violence. Freedom does not mean we can do whatever we want, but it is guaranteed in the range of the responsibility that can be shouldered.

4-6. "Thought of remorse" of truth and "thought of grudge" of fact

I could say that all theories and rules in the PARAREVO theory are based on the "thought of remorse." Those who live the way of PARAREVO understand that they must make the paradigm revolution of the existing purpose and value of life, and try to change the "thought of grudge" to the "thought of remorse," which is the important equation to graduate from the earth star.

Both remorse and grudge are the thoughts of hard feelings toward one's own mind, however, the meaning of its nature is totally opposite. The "thought of grudge" is the root of the mind, and the "thought of remorse" is to feel the mind. The "thought of grudge" is the one derived from the root of the instinctive survival consciousnesses based on the rule of "body is subjective and spirit is objective," and it's also directed to victim consciousness and the shifting of responsibility, based on unpleasant feelings dominated by physical desires. The "thought of remorse" is the one derived from the root of SHINSEI, based on the rule of "spirit is subjective and body is objective," and it's also directed to the wrongdoer consciousness and the principle of Self-responsibility which accept everything with modesty, humility, and gratitude and joy by regretting deep sin and poor mind of oneself with penitence.

It is because the earth star is the prison planet, and perceiving the earth star in the infinite universe, it is nothing more than the position of the prisoner. That is, *as seen from the universal dimension, there are only wrongdoers with deep sin but no victims at all on the earth star.* From this point of view, evaluating, blaming, or judging others is more insignificant than human beings judging that this bacterium is good but that virus is bad. It is very low for prisoners to blame and judge other prisoners. When you understand things from the point of view of the universal dimension and evoke your consciousness, there is a huge difference in the spiritual dimension compared with the point of view at the earth level dimension.

People who are in the non-PARAREVO world are made fools of by the instinctive survival consciousnesses, and only live their life to live for living even though they know they will die eventually, and end their precious and valuable life for the physical world benefits, like ants and cockroaches being preoccupied by only the immediate future.

Those who live the way of PARAREVO are not caught up in the immediate future. They always direct the consciousness to the infinite universe existing as the undeniable fact, and try to consider deeply why they are living such an inconvenient life on the earth star which is like a dust particle in the universe. They understand

Chapter Four ☆ The Conclusion

what their role and responsibility on the prison star is, and try to live with the "thought of remorse," based on the wrongdoer consciousness and the principle of Self-responsibility.

The fundamental theory and the rule of the "thought of remorse" laid the foundation of the PARAREVO theory. The PARAREVO theory defines that *the existence of the consciousness based on SHINSEI is truth, so that it is to expel the "body mind," which exists as the physical desire and the relative objectivity, according to the principle of dimensional integration by internal separation, to direct to the "soul mind," which exists as the consciousness of the soul and the relative subjectivity, and to complete Self-Enlightenment and spiritual evolution by sublimating each step of the spiritual dimension in order to graduate from the earth star.*

The "thought of grudge" is explained like this. People who are made fools of with the external evaluation based on the fact, and expel the "soul mind" which exists as the intention of the soul, according to the principle of dimensional domination based on external separation, and direct to the "body mind" which exists as desires and attachments of the physical body, are giving up the responsibility for the assignment, which is to release ONSHU by loving ONSHU. They fall into victim consciousness and shift responsibility by Self-defense, and repeat the rule of reincarnation many times.

A simple example of a phenomenon for the principle of dimensional domination by external separation based on the "thought of grudge" is the paradox of *the Atonement of Jesus on the cross,* which is interpreted in the totally opposite way. Let`s verify the basis of the words of Jesus on the cross: "Lord, please forgive them" toward the

Jewish and Roman soldiers. Since the truth of Jesus exists in the consciousness and the motivation based on SHINSEI, he clearly put himself in the position of the victim, and was executed because of innocent sin, by the "thought of grudge," so in his own consciousness, they were the wrongdoers to execute him even though he was innocent. Otherwise, he should definitely not have said "Lord, please forgive them," concluding that Jewish and Roman soldiers were criminal. So, he fell into victim consciousness according to the principle of dimensional domination by external separation based on the theory of good or bad, gave up the responsibility for the assignment for his Self-defense, and shifted responsibility by forcing the sin to the Jewish nation and Roman soldiers.

The "thought of grudge" is a symbol of thoughtless acts to direct the arrow of the consciousness to the outside, to give up the responsibility for one's assignment falling in to victim consciousness shifting the responsibility for Self-defense, lose *the good truth* by being made fools of by fact, and to bear a grudge to others.

The PARAREVO theory clearly defines the philosophical theory and the mental theory based on the "thought of remorse," in order to complete Self-Enlightenment and spiritual evolution directing from Homo sapiens to a higher spiritual dimension as Homo philosophical, and the even higher level of Homo cosmology, so it is very important to learn the method to grasp the fact and direct to the truth.

The "thought of remorse" is to direct the arrow of the consciousness to oneself, and to recognize all phenomena as the result of reflected fact by the projector called the cause. Since the problem and the assignment are connoted in us, we always direct the feeling of repentance to ourselves because of the manifestations of our imperfection, poor mind, deep sin, vulgarity and our ugliness, as the result. Even though the fact seems that we are the victim, we should direct to the "soul mind," by *the principle of dimensional integration by internal separation,* and complete by ourselves, Self-Enlightenment and spiritual evolution with SHINSEI integration consciousness to accept as we are unconditionally and totally with gratitude and happiness, according to the equation of releasing our own ONSHU ("body mind") by loving ONSHU.

Therefore, those who live the way of PARAREVO understand that all things that happened in this world are fact being manifested by the cause, the problem, and the assignment, connoted in themselves, whether it is good or bad, so that they never empathize or vent their feelings to the outside carelessly. The PARAREVO theory clarifies the role and the responsibility of the assignment for the life of wrongdoer and victim by truth, and understands that the assignment responsibility of the victim is bigger and heavier than that of the wrongdoer. It is because victim consciousness is easier to fall into and become a brutal person, who is going to the spiritual world holding poor ONSHU, and will descend to this world again as a brutal person, according to the rule of reincarnation.

4-7. Verification of the way of life of Jesus and the way of life of PARAREVO

I would like to verify the truth of the way of life of Jesus and the truth of the way of life of PARAREVO. Why had the view of life and death of Jesus on the cross, as the poor spiritual dimension, been lifted to the Messiah as the substitute for God?

I would also like to verify the fundamental difference between *the way of life of Jesus* and *the way of life of PARAREVO* by comparing the Atonement theory that expiated all sins of human beings by the Crucifixion of Jesus, with the PRAREVO theory.

On the cross, Jesus showed his affliction to God and appealed by asking as "Eli Eli la`ma sa bach tha`ni? My God, My God, why have you forsaken me?" It seems Jesus was just an ordinary person up to this point, when you consider the spiritual dimension of his consciousness. However, at the next moment, he said that "Father, forgive them, for they know not what they do." So, the existence of the phenomenon based on things, had been formed in front of the public, which is the fact that *Jesus was crucified on the cross and died.* Whether he was guilty or not was left to the relative evaluation and judgment of each person, and whether it was the fact or not, it had no meaning or significance for Jesus, who was dying.

The truth of Jesus existed on his consciousness based on SHINSEI when he was on the cross. The exercise of the consciousness and the motivation of the words "Father, forgive them" showed that he obviously crossed the separation border line between himself and others, directed the arrow of the consciousness to them (the external existence) and made the fact that distinguished clearly between good and bad according to the theory of good and bad, considered him as the Messiah on the side of goodness, and the Jewish nations and Roman soldiers as criminals, belonged to the Satan side.

I think that Jesus arrogantly made others out to be criminals and gave up the principle of Self-responsibility toward the cause, problem, and assignment connoted in him, and left the world playing

Chapter Four ☆ The Conclusion

the role as the only son of God, without any repentance, modesty or humility. The truth of the way of life of Jesus was to distinguish the object of evil to the outside and blame others, and develop the victim consciousness and the theory of shifting responsibility, according to the "principle of dimensional domination" by external separation based on the "thought of grudge" based on the Self-defense that he was not bad. With two irresponsible words by Jesus, "forgive them," which was I think totally not his business, he made himself look as if he was the victim of the only son of God, and directed human beings to the position of wrongdoer, according to *the principle of dimensional domination by external separation* with the external evaluation of good and bad toward the outside, and shifting responsibility to them, resulting in his own victim consciousness. It also became the source of religious struggles and religious wars in the Christian history.

By this theory of good and bad, Jesus played the role of his own scenario to have himself as the Messiah (the Savior), and as a result made human beings shoulder the debt, being caught in their own trap by directing to poor consciousness, and making them fall victim to the inconvenience called *"spiritual Self-trapping,"* by directing the Christian followers to the religious spell. Jesus made the third party, human beings, intervening in the relationship between Jesus and God, and formed the corruption structure called the triangle system of confusion.

Truth exists in the pair system called the existence of the consciousness based on SHINSEI, so that at the moment the third party intervenes, the principle of Self-responsibility is lost, and inevitably we will be directed to victim consciousness shifting responsibility, dominated by the theory of good or bad and the theory of superiority or inferiority, and end up in the evil competition principle.

Christianity has continuously proven in its history of struggles and wars that the evil competition principles only produce struggle and destruction, and do not solve anything. Because of the false and untrue theory of the Atonement of Jesus, the ghost of Jesus and Christian followers have been forced to rely on each other by the rule of the relative original power based on the mind and the spirit, for two thousand years, and the path to *the independent type of salvation* by Self-effort has been closed, and Jesus himself has been spiritually bound by the consciousness and the piety of Christian followers, and has not been allowed to go to the spiritual world, could not re-descend by the rule of reincarnation, and because of his ignorance he has elected by himself to continue existing as the residual haunting on the earth star. Until Christian followers are completely gone, the soul and the spirit of Jesus will continue to be bound on the earth.

It means that when we depend on Jesus and pray to him, we will be dominated by Jesus. Please remember the rule of the universe is nonaggression and nonintervention, so that it is for us to save ourselves. At the same time, what is worse is Jesus is bound by desires of believers and his soul will remain on the ground of the earth. The more we worship and depend on him, the more difficult it becomes for his soul to release. We should free this vicious circle of co-depends by our love toward Jesus and begin walking the path to independence. Jesus looked for love and preached love but on the cross, his love remained in a range of external evaluation of good

Chapter Four ☆ The Conclusion

and bad saying that they were wrong but he was right. However, if we really think about him, we should stop asking forgiveness from him and start taking care of ourselves by ourselves as an independent type of salvation.

In order to guarantee the rule of freedom, the rule of the universe makes each person secure the principle of Self-responsibility. If the value of security is big enough, such as when you have no choice but to accept a difficult problem unconditionally and totally with gratitude and joy, you are going to obtain a large degree of acceptance of love and the degree of freedom of the consciousness when you overcome the problem. Therefore, the universe would not forgive or punish anybody, but would carry through the principle of nonaggression and nonintervention. All causes, problems and assignments are connoted in the person, and manifested facts should be overcome by the principle of Self-responsibility by the truth of the person.

Since people who live the way of PARAREVO understand that the greatest meaning and significance for their Self-Enlightenment and spiritual evolution to make Self-completion based on the principle of Self-responsibility toward all facts by the existence of the consciousness based on SHINSEI, they never fall into victim consciousness and shift responsibility by crossing the separation border line between themselves and others. They also understand that things which happened as poor phenomena are the shadow of the truth that their own spiritual dimension was low because of their own sinful, poor and vulgar mind, and it became fact. So they direct the consciousness to unconditional acceptance as *necessity is necessary goodness,* with penitence based on the "thought of remorse," and achieve Self-completion to gratitude and happiness with *thanks for the difficult problems.*

If those who live the way of PARAREVO are placed in the same position as Jesus, they would transcend the death on the cross by saying "To SHINSEI inside me, since this cross is the cause, the problem, and the assignment connoted in my own soul, it has nothing to do with others. As you accept me unconditionally and totally, I accept this cross unconditionally and totally with gratitude and happiness." In this way, they direct to SHINSEI integration consciousness by the pair system of SHINSEI and themselves, according to the principle of dimensional integration by internal separation, without violating the separation border line between themselves and others, achieve Self-completion to direct to Self-Enlightenment and spiritual evolution, according to the true view of life and death based on the rule of "the attainment of the spiritual being during life," without making the third party intervene, and by carrying out the principle of Self-responsibility, and open the path to graduation from the earth star.

In the PARAREVO theory, the direction toward separation between goodness and badness is clearly distinguished by *the external separation based on the "thought of grudge"* and *the internal separation based on the "thought of remorse."* External separation is the thought to develop the theory of good and bad toward the outside of oneself, and internal separation is the thought to develop the theory of good and bad toward the "soul mind" and the "body mind" in oneself. Therefore, they never fall into victim consciousness and shift the responsibility toward others, never cross the separation border line between themselves and others, or develop the theory of good and bad toward the outside based on the *"thought of grudge."*

The concept of the theory of the Atonement of Jesus on the cross and the concept of spiritual evolution of the PARAREVO theory are directed to totally opposite theoretical frameworks and values based on the cosmic philosophy. The way of life of PARAREVO proposes the essence for the way of life as Homo cosmology, but not as Homo philosophical, based on the rule of "spirit is subjective and body is objective."

4-8. Logos for the way of life of PARAREVO

The essence of the way of life of "SHINSEI integration consciousness" based on the PARAREVO theory is made clear by the Logos. And *The Logos for the way of life of PARAREVO* is as follows. *By drawing the separation border line between now and past or future, and between you and me, and establishing Self-integration with SHINSEI integration consciousness to accept as they are unconditionally and totally with gratitude and happiness, direct the universal Self-creation eternally which manifests free individual art based on love.*

In this Logos, the universal truth and rule are expressed simply. It is because the PARAREVO theory is not suggesting nonsensical, impossible and unreasonable demands, but is setting the paradigm that anybody can actualize their own Self-Enlightenment and spiritual evolution by Self-effort based on free intention. If this paradigm is only recognized as ideal theory, it is because of the poorness of mind and the lowness of the spiritual dimension.

According to the principle of dimensional domination, the "soul mind" is dominated by the poor "body mind" and directed to corruption leading only to Self-hatred and Self-legitimacy by Self-escape.

The mind of human beings is always wavering in the slight fluctuation of imperfection between the "soul mind" and the "body mind" based on the rule of entropy relativity. The PARAREVO theory has a base in the universal fundamental truth which *directs to Self-determination with Self-management and Self-completion by Self-responsibility, based on the rule of freedom.* No matter what the fact is, whether it completes to gratitude and happiness by the relative original power with SHINSEI and the "soul mind," or completes to uncomfortable feelings by the relative original power with SHINSEI and the "body mind," is up to the free intention of oneself, and the truth is led to Self-management toward Self-determination and Self-completion by Self-responsibility.

In the Logos of the way of life of PARAREVO, all things will be possible with the Self-effort to direct the spiritual dimension to a higher level, by free intention of oneself and the creation of joy based on love.

Now, I would like to distinguish and explain clearly, difference between truth and fact of the Logos of the way of life of PARAREVO, one by one.

4-9. Truth is in now and fact is in time axis

The necessity to live in the "Now" is because we will complete truth based on the rule of preservation by inscription, which is that we should live with the subconscious more than the original existing consciousness, which is the experience consciousness in the past, and live with the emerging consciousness more than the subconscious, further more we live in the "Now" with SHINSEI integration consciousness more than the emerging consciousness.

It is because if we live in the past and the future we will stray from the zero time period, the "Now," so our consciousness of now would be dominated by delusion and illusion, which is based on the fact of the past, and it will take us farther from the truth. I call the present or the Now *"real time"* and the past and the future on the time axis is called *"virtual time."*

Since the fundamental way of life of PARAREVO is directing spiritual evolution based on the rule of "spirit is subjective and body is objective," PARAREVO people try to release the domination of the time axis, such as the fact in the past and the future exist in the image called memories of the brain, based on the rule of "body is subjective and spirit is objective," and aim to the way of life of truth, which completes in the Now. It is because *even though fact exists on the time axis, truth does not exist there.* Truth exists in the digital world, which is *the real-time* of the moment, the Now. The time axis, which is fact, exists is the ghost world with delusion and illusion, and the future is the demon world with anxiety and fear. Based on the rule of entropy relativity, if the existence of the past is denied, the existence of the future is denied also and only the "Now" is affirmed.

Since the PARAREVO theory strictly follows *existentialism,* only truth called *the Now* is affirmed. *The Now is a point and zero time period.* Since in the zero time period, all things are completed in the continuity of the point called the Now, the time axis does not exist there. The Now is the beginning and ending for everything, and the point of true moment. Thus, *the zero time period is the only universal dimension which achieves the dimensional integration for all things in the whole universe, and converts and preserves digitally by the rule of preservation by inscription.*

No matter whether it exists in the lower dimension or the higher dimension, the Now itself exists and completes to the zero time period as dimensional integration. Therefore, the universe is forced to exist by accepting as they are, unconditionally and totally in the Now, the zero time period of the moment. This is the reason why Alpha is Omega, the beginning is the ending, the cause is the result, and a presence has a shape but does not have a shape. Like this, the contradictory things exist and disappear in the digital world, synchronically and simultaneously. This is called the zero time period, or the Now. After passing one minute, and even one second, there only exists the world of the consciousness of supposition and speculation by false image (virtual) of delusions and illusions. *SHINSEI shoulders the entire responsibility for the world of the consciousness of real image (reality) of the zero time period of the moment, the Now, and accepts only the truth, unconditionally and totally.*

Our soul, the spiritual consciousness entity, is restrained by the time axis with the concept of memories, which are created by the brain, and we are forced to an inconvenient existence. The universe exists in each spiritual dimension by the relative universal original power, and the whole universe is being dimensionally integrated and converted digitally to newer information, at the zero time period by the rule of preservation by inscription, and it directs to the higher level by continuous now, and is preserved digitally, and with the sustainable mechanism, the harmony and the order are directed eternally, and prepare the system which makes it possible to exist progressively and permanently. For us, *the truth is that we can live by the relative original power between SHINSEI and the spiritual consciousness entity, and the fact is that we are alive by the relative original power between the spiritual consciousness entity and the body at the moment.*

Since in the PARAREVO theory, only truth exists in the zero time period, the "Now," the innermost secret for the way of life of PARAREVO is to not bring untruth in the attitude of life. In order to do so, we should not empathize to the past and the future with delusion and illusion, which do not exist, and live in the truth by following existentialism in *the Now*. Thus, the PARAREVO theory advises that if we are captured in the past and the future, we are not able to discover any meaning or significance, so religions show their concept nicely by the rule of causality of the body, but are considered all untruths.

4-10. Life is with Self-determination and Self-responsibility

Our consciousness should not live in the past or the future by the domination of the time axis. Therefore, if you want to live your life recklessly in the Now by the physical domination of the excessive physical world benefits in the center, you will be dominated by the time axis, and would be caught in the past and the future. On the other hand, if you want to live for the spiritual benefits for the spiritual evolution as the purpose of life, you consider that the "Now" is precious and valuable and you should live in the "Now." Unpleasant feelings are brought by delusion and illusion of the past and the future. The ownership and the right for management of your life are given and entrusted only to you.

Since the rule of the universe puts all things into your Self-determination and Self-responsibility due to freedom and quality, you should not transfer the ownership and the right for management of your life to others by their lead and control of words. However, sadly, human beings are weak, so we often fall into dependence condition called "parasite syndrome," and give up the principle of Self-responsibility, shifting the responsibility to others and asking for salvation and help. Because of this weakness, we are taken advantage of and end up choosing inconvenient life by ourselves. Since the rule of salvation is only works by own self, asking for salvation and help by others is nonsense.

Devils of ghosts carrying grudges and hard feelings exist in the past, and the devils of delusion and illusion, such as anxiety and fear, exist in the future. Therefore, the SHINSEI inside of you called truth, and oneself, collectively called SHINSEI integrated consciousness entity, exist at the zero time period, the "Now."

We should have courage to achieve Self-completion by Self-determination with Self-responsibility for *the Now*, with a persistent and resolute attitude. Then, you can live easily, by accepting yourself unconditionally and complete the propriety of all things by the way of life of PARAREVO. We should understand that living not in the present causes us to retreat to the past and makes it impossible to create evolution and development.

This problem is expanding from the individual level to the national and global level. For example, many countries still bring up the history of the past and insist that the terrible things which happened were the responsibility others. When they still live in the past of an unhappy era, prosperous diplomatic reconciliation is never possible due to grudge and hatred, and it makes it impossible for realization of the collaboration world, the most precious world, with co-existence, symbiosis and co-promotion in the present.

Religious conflicts and ethnic conflicts are the cause of delusion and illusion from the past, and are creating ONSHU. According to the PAREVO theory, one of the roots of evil is domination of the time axis and time itself. Moreover, it is said in the PAREVO theory that if we transcend ONSHU of the past generation with love and intention to accept as they are unconditionally and totally with gratitude and happiness in this generation, and make a compromise with each other, the world of real collaboration will be fulfilled.

In short, the past and the future create unpleasant feelings to our existence and life, and because of it they invite the chain of unhappiness, build the society which increases entropy (disorder) as the negative assets in various places, and will aim to succeed to their children.

4-11. Universe is undeniable existentialism

The innermost secret to live in the actual world, the world of reality and not being dominated in the virtual world, is by drawing the separation borderline toward the time axis, which is the past and *the future. This way, we are able to live in the Now, existentially. In order to sever one's connections with and wash our hands of ghosts and demons of the past and the future, we must draw the separation borderline between ourselves and the virtual world, and manifest the realities of existential life, the Now, and live with gratitude and joy. To stick to the undeniable existentialism, the Now, is the most easygoing way of life, and it becomes the fundamental training for the spiritual life as truth and it will be meaningful and valuable for us.*

Some people might wonder and ask if we should draw the separation borderline even to good and pleasant memories of the past. I would say "Yes, we should draw the separation borderline between ourselves and all of the past, and just complete the Now." Many elderly people who miss the old days and keep grumbling that "the past was great and compared to that, the present is not so great." However, no matter how good the past was, if the present is worse, what was the life for? If the present is the best, you would never say the old days were great. By the principle of a sign of inequality, if the present is the best, the past lost the luster even if it was actually a happy life, so you would not mention past anymore, because it will be erased by the rule of preservation by inscription, inevitably.

The life should be more wonderful and happier today than yesterday, a year ago, fifteen years ago, or even thirty years ago, otherwise, there is no meaning or significance to live in the present by SHINSEI. If the past was the best and now is the worst, your whole life becomes the worst by the rule of preservation by inscription.

Those who live the way of PARAREVO always try to ask themselves, "which time was the more wonderful for you, yesterday or today?" They would never want to say that the past was great because it is against SHINSEI, which is living together with them, so they would answer themselves by saying today is the best, and try to live the way of life of truth to complete the Now with gratitude and joy.

We would only bear Self-responsibility toward Self-determination to *the Now* and accept it unconditionally and totally with gratitude and happiness. We do not have to be dominated by the ghosts of the past and the demons of the future. It is because to live in *the Now* will be the most important factor for establishing Self-integration.

If there is one truth, which is able to cross the separation borderline and make Self-completion, it will be love. If you emphasize and vent the feeling toward all objects by the consciousness other than love, you would definitely fall into unpleasant feelings. Therefore, to live in *the Now* based on free love, existentially, will become the basis of the way of PARAREVO.

4-12. Truth, the innermost secret to live in the Now

Although the concept to live in the Now is mentioned convincingly in the mental world and religious world, since they are caught by the past facts such as the scriptures and the Bible, it is hard to say that they are really living in the Now. When people are told, blindly, to live in the Now is the best way, it is never mentioned how to do that. Without finding the existing purpose and value, there is no meaning or significance to live in the Now.

In order to live in the Now, the paradigm and the concept must be established. I could say that *the ignorance is a shadow of death, and does not produce any emotion. Life then, is only a word and is actually the same as being dead.*

The rule of the universe is based on the rule of entropy relativity, and the opposite things are directed to a higher spiritual dimension and are evolving, according to the principle of dimensional integration, relatively, synchronically, and simultaneously, by the relative original power with the slight fluctuation of imperfection. The existing purpose and the existing value of the universe open the path of the feelings relatively based on love, and are directed to Self-completion with joy, together. Therefore, living in the Now, alone, does not have any meaning or significance.

In order to live in the Now, we should establish Self-integrity to complete with joy to all objects we relate to, based on love. For human beings, the best relative existence of the "negative" and the "positive" is women and men. There exists no other rule of the "negative" and the "positive" of the relative love on the earth. This is called the "rule of pair system of love." The best preparation for the moment of death to go to the spiritual world of the universe (cosmic world) is for women and men to convert their consciousness digitally to *the Now,* which is completed to joy synchronically and simultaneously based on free love, by the rule of preservation by inscription, and *preserve the feelings of love and joy.* The spiritual world of the universe (cosmic world) is the world higher than the earth dimension, beyond the range of reincarnation in the tangible and intangible earth.

However, just living in the Now does not have any meaning. In order for us to complete the existing meaning and existing value to live in the Now in preparation for "Heaven," is to co-exist with somebody we love and co-promote happiness by the rule of pair system of love.

It is impossible to complete love alone, even for the saints and righteous persons. In order to complete love, it requires women who represent the "negative" (half of the universe) and the relative subjectivity, and men who represent the "positive" (the other half of the universe) and the relative objectivity. The men's theory of power, domination, struggle and destruction, needs to be comprehended and integrated by the women's theory of love, integration, harmony and creation, according to the principle of dimensional integration. So, it is necessary to find an ideal partner of love in order to complete love.

4-13. The rule of "spirit is subjective and body is objective" will release the genetic linkage

The dietary desire changes to the material desire and the sexual desire changes to the dominating desire, and both desires, as the instinctive remaining consciousnesses, are surviving in us still now on this planet, as our instinctive desire consciousnesses. As long as the life entities continue to exist on this earth star, the instinctive desire consciousnesses continue to exist as the instinctive remaining consciousnesses by the genetic domination while achieving the dimensional ascent. They are the fatal genetic dominating consciousnesses.

The trials of mental and physical pain are the best chance

for us to achieve spiritual evolution, by releasing the instinctive remaining consciousness of physical domination, because you would never wish to graduate from the earth star if you are blessed with the physical world benefits. But if you have to live a miserable and unhappy life in penance and hardship, then you would wish to be released from this world by taking off the body as soon as possible and never want to come back to the earth star again. As you can see from those examples, whether you live in this world with the physical world benefits and just enjoy the earth life or whether you chose a life with the trials and aim for spiritual evolution is up to your determination. Spiritual evolution is led for the truth of each person, which is Self-management by Self-determination and Self-completion by Self-responsibility based on the rule of freedom.

For example, if there were truth and fact regarding the atonement of Jesus on the cross, it would only exist in *the Now* of Jesus on the cross, because he was responsible for each moment of how he lived and how he died. When Jesus was placed in the poor environment, facing death, there was significance and value on what Jesus said and did at the zero time period, and he made, by Self-determination, the position in the spiritual dimension to go after death by the truth of his emotional world and personality dimension at the moment of the verge of life and death.

In order to release the desire consciousness of the body which it has inherited continuously according to the rule of the genetic chain based on the rule of causality of the body, we have to live by accepting now which is the corpus of the history, unconditionally, with the rule of "spirit is subjective and body is objective."

4-14. The PARAREVO theory shows the "rule of the attainment of the spiritual being during life"

Even Jesus and Kukai (the founder of Shingon-shu, one of the Buddhism groups in Japan) were obsessed with and paid particular attention to the physical death based on the earth logical evidence, however, with such a sense of value, it is not possible to surpass and release the physical domination.

The true way of the life entity is that the life and the death are completed as appearing and disappearing at the same time, synchronically and simultaneously by the relative original power, the slight fluctuation of imperfection between SHINSEI and the soul, based on the cosmological evidence. In the universe, nothing remains the same for even one moment. The true way of the life entity works this way. The conflicting life and death are converted digitally to *the life,* the relative subjectivity at the zero time period, the Now, and *the death,* the relative objectivity, is deleted, then new *life* is preserved digitally, by the rule of preservation by inscription, so this becomes the sustainable system for the soul, the spiritual consciousness entity, to exist eternally.

According to the PARAREVO theory, we are living but at the same time we are dying, and we are dying but at the same time we are living. It is because the death of prenatal life produces the life on the earth, and the death on the earth produces the life in the spiritual world. The world where the system of the time axis in this world is compressed to the zero time period, is the view of life and death of the digital world of the spiritual consciousness entity, as the intangible substantial world and released from the physical domination. Thus, neither the life nor the death is first, it is just directed to the life in the slight fluctuation of imperfection between the life and the death, so that a new life is born by death. By this rule, it is possible for the soul to exist eternally. Our spiritual consciousness entity is the synchronous existence of death and life. This rule is called, by the PARAREVO theory, *the "rule of the attainment of the spiritual being during life."*

This rule is explained as follows. All lives shouldering the physical body are able to complete the spiritual consciousness entity beyond the body, according to the principle of dimensional integration based on the rule of "spirit is subjective and body is objective." Therefore, regarding the true life entity in the intangible substantial world, the life and the death of the spiritual life entity also derive and disappear simultaneously and synchronically at each moment of zero time based on the rule of entropy relativity, and will be completed to new life by the rule of preservation by inscription.

Those who live the way of PARAREVO are never captured and attached to the physical life which shoulders the fate to die, so they never bring anxiety and fear toward the death of the body in the present, based on the true view of life and death. Thus, even though they shoulder the body in this world, they can draw the separation borderline between the spiritual consciousness entity and the physical body, and can live by being superintended by the death of the body. As long as we are not controlled by the body, it is the same as not having a body. The "soul mind" and the "body mind" exist naturally. However, if we are not controlled by the "body mind" and it does not evoke the "body mind" in our consciousness, it is the same as the "body mind" does not exist. The ordinary view of life

Chapter Four ☆ The Conclusion

and death in this world is based on the rule of "body is subjective and spirit is objective," being controlled by the body and clinging to the life in this world. So we are directed to seek only the physical world benefits and end our lifetime with just that.

Those who live the way of life of PARAREVO establish the true view of life and death, so if they are suddenly diagnosed with an incurable disease and are informed by a doctor that they are dying, they will accept it unconditionally and totally with gratitude and happiness, by the "rule of the attainment of the spiritual being during life."

When the truth of your spiritual dimension becomes higher and larger, the reality and problems of this world become lower and smaller. On the other hand, when the truth of the spiritual dimension becomes lower and smaller, the hurdle of reality becomes higher, and the problems of this world get larger and more difficult to deal with. For example, when the existence purpose and value of the life in your consciousness, based on SHINSEI, becomes higher and larger based on the faith to graduate from the earth star, the existence of the earth itself becomes lower and smaller. When your consciousness is occupied with only the immediate future, without the purpose of life, the reality will be a huge existence.

In the intangible substantial world, the moment you have a thought, things will be completed and disappear immediately by truth. Since in this world, there is the time axis existing in the physical domination, it takes time and distance for the things you think to be manifested, and obviously separation interval, the time axis, and the distance interval take place before reaching to the cause and effect and the life and death.

If Kukai, Japanese Buddhist, and Jesus had embraced the "rule of the attainment of the spiritual being during life," they would not have selected the path of penance and hardship and the trials and tribulations for releasing the physical domination, by being caught in the existence of the body and death. As a matter of course, Kukai and many other Japanese Buddhists would not select the path to the "attainment of the Buddhahood during life," training themselves like a suicide act, because it did not produce any meaning or significance.

People who consider committing suicide believe that all their problems are gone after dying, so they would be relieved because everything is over, and make the action to commit suicide, however, since they are the presence of the "rule of the attainment of the spiritual being during life," in which they are dying during living and are alive during dying, so after committing suicide they only lose their physical body but nothing would change at all as far as their spiritual situation, and it invites the result accompanied with more pain by being a bounded soul on the earth.

It is because the true view of life and death *is based on the rule of "spirit is subjective and body is objective," so whether you are in this world or in the spiritual world, the life entity has the system which will be enable it to exist eternally, by the sustainable mechanism by the "rule of the attainment of the spiritual being during life."* The existing purpose and the existing value are not for the view of life and death of the body restricted in this world, but they exist for the moment of death to achieve spiritual evolution of the life entity to a higher spiritual dimension, and continue to live in the spiritual world digitally.

Chapter Four ☆ The Conclusion

Since the level of the spiritual world is determined at the moment of your physical death, you must accept death whenever it comes. It is the way of life that is directed to the original cosmological evidence to live in truth based on the "rule of the attainment of the spiritual being during life," Self-completing each moment, in the Now, with gratitude and happiness by the way of life of PARAREVO.

The Logos to release the original existence consciousness is this. "Dear SHINSEI, as you accept me unconditionally, I accept all instinctive survival consciousnesses existing inside me." It is not more than that and not less than that.

4-15. The rule of genetic linkage will lead to unhealthy dependence and shift responsibility to others

The theory of lineage causality of retribution in Buddhism is a theoretical system of the physical category based on the rule of "body is subjective and spirit is objective." It is the theory based on DNA, which is the common denominator for the terrestrial life, which I think is the pretense theory of untruth and deceit, extremely reversing the order of importance toward the evolutionary theory.

The genetic information, which had been inherited through DNA continuously in the history of the physical evolution of 3.8 billion years from the primitive life entity, has internalized into the structural arrangement of genes of our 60 trillion cells, and information of our ancestors of 3.8 billion years exists and is still alive in our body, as an undeniable fact at the moment of the Now. However, what we inherited from our ancestors is genetic information of the physical evolution based on the rule of "body is subjective and spirit is objective," but not the soul, the spiritual consciousness entity. Since our soul and ancestors do not have any relation, *descendent does not exist because of the ancestors.* The spiritual consciousness entity which became a child, determined the parents and the genes and descended by conception, based on the rule of "spirit is subjective and body is objective." Consequently, the linage has continued to exist.

No matter how much a couple wishes to have a child, if the existence and the determination of the soul which would become the child would not be ready in the spiritual world, the linage in this world would be terminated. In other words, nobody in this world is given the right to choose the life and the lineage.

Even if it is a test-tube baby or artificial insemination, the mechanism and the system of the conception descent is the same. Parents do not have the cause and the subjectivity of the lineage, but it is left to the spiritual consciousness entity which exists in the spiritual world and would become the child. Regarding the soul of ancestors, only the principle of Self-responsibility by Self-determination of the ancestors themselves exists. So, there is no cause or responsibility toward descendants.

It is fine if you like to hold memorial services for merely Self-satisfaction. However, even though you hold memorial services, it only makes the religious groups happy. So, you should not waste your emotions, time, and money for the virtual world (imaginary world). Instead, you should make Self-effort for the realization of loving and ideal family and society, by building ideal family relationships and society relationships, treating each other tenderly, loving each other, understanding each other, and promoting each other existentially by directing yourself to truth, as the existence of the consciousness based on SHINSEI in "the Now," the actual world.

4-16. Self-integration in the thought of child and parents

"You guys made me by your own decision. I didn`t ask to be born." These are the words of children when they have a fight with their parents; however, this is totally wrong. From the point of view of the parents, it sounds like bitter words, but they could say that "you were the one who came to this world by yourself. We did not ask for you to come." That might be appropriate based on the rule of "spirit is subjective and body is objective."

I believe that the parents are the ones who should be thankful and accept the fact, unconditionally, that the child is the one who went through all the trouble of selecting the parents. People who live the way of life of PARAREVO are sure to say on the birthday of their children "Happy Birthday to you! Thanks for choosing us, who are in the lower spiritual dimension, as your parents. We would like to toast for your courage to pick us." They would pay their respects to the children.

Have you ever considered whether you are a person in the higher spiritual dimension with suitable personality and spirituality to be selected as a parent? Since children and descendants have made the decision to select their parents and ancestors for the spiritual evolution in the history of each period according to the rule of reincarnation based on the rule of preservation by inscription, the children and the descendants have the responsibility for their life. Since parents have not sufficiently educated their children about this throughout history, and have neglected the Self-effort for spiritual evolution, human beings have been made fools of by the rule of the genetic chain based on the wrong rule of physical causality, which is to get priorities mixed up, and being dominated by the religious doctrines with the paradoxical theory of "body is subjective and spirit is objective," have built untrue religious cultures and dependence on those religions. As a result, we keep the old-fashioned ideas and shift responsibility to parents and others.

Also, there are many children and descendants who are not able to be independent and are unable to complete Self-responsibility, so they cannot achieve the paradigm revolution to the spiritual evolution in order to acquire true freedom. So they have delayed the history of spiritual evolution. Because of this, the concept of "it is accepted because they are parent-child" was established, and human beings have added this concept to the core of ONSHU. As a result, parents have shouldered a bigger burden toward the children, and the children have built sorrow and ONSHU toward the parents leaving a huge blemish in the personality formation history.

By making theoretical conversion from the paradigm of causality of "parent-child ideology" based on the rule of "body is subjective and spirit is objective," to the paradoxical theory of the paradigm of causality of "child-parent ideology" based on the rule of "spirit is subjective and body is objective." By the PARAREVO theory which is "not accepted because they are parent-child," it is important that we should become independent by the principle of Self-responsibility in order to complete love, release the burden and ONSHU of each parent and child, and direct to Self-Enlightenment and spiritual evolution.

4-17. The Now will release causality under the time axis

Human beings should not be dominated by deceit and the untrue theory of causality of physical domination, which is the theory of retribution according to the rule of "body is subjective and spirit is objective." Instead, we should make Self-completion by directing to memories of the soul of a higher level, by the rule of preservation by inscription, based on the "rule of the attainment of the spiritual being during life" which is to live in "the Now" by the PARAREVO theory.

Based on the cosmological evidence, we could have shortened the time axis to the new era, in high speed with the completion of things in every moment, and restore to the zero time period, and achieve spiritual evolution to a higher level rapidly, by reducing labor.

It means that we should have been able to compress the time axis domination to the zero time period, the Now, and shorten the time for evolution. Therefore, we should be released from the theory of the rule of physical causality, in which we are caught in our own trap by the past cause, and we should be released from all religions and make Self-completion of the spiritual evolution to acquire true independence and freedom.

4-18. Life is based on the rule of Self-responsibility

The rule of the universe is led to Self-determination and Self-responsibility based on the rule of freedom, and achieves Self-completion, without being dependent on anything or dominated by anything according to the principle of nonaggression and nonintervention. Therefore, everything is equal.

In the spiritual world we have made the assignments and scenario for Self-Enlightenment in this world, by ourselves, based on our spiritual dimension, and determined our parents and life. Then we descended by conception, selecting the fertilized egg of the mother, in order to make Self-completion of the responsibility of assignment for spiritual evolution, according to the "rule of reincarnation."

Our spiritual dimension will be determined at the moment of physical death, by how we lived in this world. If the soul can redeem after death by having a grand funeral service and lots of praying, what is the significant meaning of life in this world? *This world is for the preparation period to go to the spiritual world, so since that period is over when you die, it is already too late to do anything.* If conditions change after death, difficulties and efforts in this world will have no meaning, and the rule of reincarnation itself will be destroyed. It is up to you if you perform a funeral service and have a priest or monk pray for the courtesy or debt feeling for deceased people; it is comforting for each other and for Self-satisfaction. However, I think, it takes unnecessary time and money, and increases anxiety.

Anyway, in order to release your own ONSHU by yourself, you must make Self-determination of the parents and Self-completion of releasing ONSHU toward the parents, based on the rule of freedom, then it will become possible to release the historical ONSHU of the "parent-child." Shifting the responsibility to others, such as the parents and ancestors, means to escape from Self-responsibility and abandon the assignment.

However, the rule of causality of the religious groups, as in Buddhism, shifts the responsibility to ancestors who have no way of knowing about the problems, between you and your father-in-law or mother-in-law, or between wife and husband, and the problems with children. But they are switching problem consciousness to those ONSHU existing near you, guiding you to easier choices, making it convenient to avoid Self-responsibility and make Self-escape, and Self-entrapment by untruth and descent theory, and connect you to the spell of religious dependence. You won't reach any solution at all even if you abandon your role and responsibility and shift your responsibility to others. Most of those who have love lacking syndrome in the lower spiritual dimension, such as weak or poor parent-child relationship, or are unable to surpass their parents-in-law by love, are easy to fall into religious dependence.

4-19. Addiction to religion is similar to schizophrenia

It is an undeniable *fact* that the fundamental ideas of religions, such as the Bible, Islamic or Buddhist scriptures and sutras, are *the existence of phenomena based on things* which are relics of the past. Although the Bible, sutras and scriptures are only one fact, many religions and religious sects have been created all over the world. This is because *truth, the existence of the consciousness of people based on SHINSEI,* touched on only one fact, people who followed that original fact were all different. Even though truth exists in the consciousness based on the SHINSEI of each person, various religions and sects have been produced by different interpretations of the fact.

Therefore, we could say that "the truth does not exist in the fact" and "there is no fact better than truth." As a result, religious struggles and religious wars have continued, dominated by a curse of the theoretical framework and the value of each religion. It is fact that they have carried ONSHU by different religious visions and Self-righteous interpretations, in the past.

Only a hundred or so years ago, there was the Edo period in Japan when samurai wore a Japanese sword on their waist for slaying people. Who could imagine such an era existed from the view of modern Japan today? Although each era has always achieved the evolution, and *the material civilization* has been rewritten to new and higher information of theoretical frameworks and values according to the rule of preservation by inscription, *religions as the mental civilization* have been made a fools of and dominated by *the fact* such as the Bible, sutra and scriptures of the past, by the time axis domination, and they have not reached to *the truth*. This is exactly *willful murder of the truth by the fact* by religions.

Religions need the Messiah and persons who have reached nirvana, as their Savior because of depravity of human progenitor in the theory of original sin, according to the poor and untrue religion theory. As a result, people appear who claim that they are the reincarnation of Buddha or the second coming of Jesus, as if they are psychic, but actually they have a destroyed personality like the schizophrenia-type gurus and wield their own interpretation of the Bible and the sutra and scriptures. They would tell about the sin of human progenitor, and sins of existing religions by the excessive crazy theory of corruption or salvation, brainwash the general public and lead them to the victim consciousness, and make them depend on the religions, by tying them with fetters to their own trap.

In many cases, mediums are the same as people with mental disorders whose chakras were destroyed. Many cult gurus are schizophrenic. They claim they are psychic but actually have strong paranoid delusions and destroyed personalities. Their followers are dominated by the guru's Self-righteous theoretical framework and values, being directed to the personality disorder of schizophrenia before they notice, by mind control, and eventually fall into Self-abandonment and isolate themselves from society. As a result, they fall into religious dependence, unable to stand by themselves, and withdraw from society. They are brainwashed to the victim consciousness which is exactly the same as people who are schizophrenic. They also tend to form an extraneous and isolated community and often intrude on the politics and/or society.

Human beings have never been depraved in the past. We have both dietary desire and sexual desire, which are the instinctive survival consciousnesses. However, dietary desire has changed to the material desire, and sexual desire has changed to the domination desire, and they continue to remain as the fate of the body. There are differences of the size and differences in dimensions, but as long as the life entities remain on the earth star, those desires remain with us.

The hidden nature of the theory of reliance upon others, such as the Messiah ideology, and the salvation ideology which is the theory that people are saved by others by the Advent thought in the termination theory and the decline of Buddhism theory. This is the nature of greedy gurus filled with property desire and domination desire. Followers are mind-controlled by anxiety and fear, being forced to an inconvenient life by following the suggestions of a guru, and many times, cause social problems such as election campaigns, by violating the border of the principle of separation of church and state. Also social crimes and selling goods claiming that the purchaser will obtain supernatural benefits.

Since the level in the spiritual world is left to Self-effort, there is absolutely no salvation by another's hand. It is because it will destroy the rule of freedom, which is the fundamental truth of the universe. The only way to go to a higher level in the spiritual world is by Self-management by Self-determination and Self-completion by Self-responsibility based on the rule of freedom. We should sublimate the steps of spiritual evolution one by one, achieving Self-Enlightenment and spirituality transformation, brightening up the spiritual consciousness entity, and lighten our own soul.

Ancestors should have opened the path to salvation by themselves by Self-responsibility. In order to not be cheated by religious groups and the mental world, we should complete the role and the responsibility to walk the independent and responsible life without depending on anything.

Here is the conclusion. The Logos to release the genetic consciousness, the indirect subconscious, are "Dear SHINSEI, as you accept me unconditionally and totally, I accepted the fact of the body in which the genetic information of all related ancestors I have, unconditionally by truth. I appreciate it."

4-20. Flashback phenomena of consciousness of past lives

According to the PARAREVO theory, the period of one cycle of reincarnation for ordinary people is about 300 years. After that the soul comes back to this world again. However, the souls which achieved reincarnation relatively quickly and descended early to this world sometimes carry over the memories of past lives up to the person's childhood. Since it is the direct experience of the soul, the feelings such as intense hatred, malice, deep-seated grudges, obsession, anxiety and fear were not able to be overwritten completely by preservation by inscription at the time of birth to this world by the rule of reincarnation, and those memories of the soul which could not be erased were sometimes brought to this world. For example, we can see the confusion of the consciousness of past life memories in the incomprehensible violent criminals and those with intense mental disorders. Panic disorder is an exact example, and recently people who suffer from it are increasing in number.

Although the person can't find the cause of the trauma in the personality formation history and there is no reason for worry and fear in the present life, suddenly anxiety and fear attack without reason from the inner consciousness, and he may suffer the symptoms of hyperventilation having chest pain with an autonomic neuropathy. These symptoms are flashback phenomenon by the consciousness of past lives. Therefore, the panic disorder is not improved unless one releases the anxiety and fear of the consciousness in the past.

In recent years, I hear of many past life therapists holding seminars and giving treatment. I cannot stop wondering about such a movement. Those are, I think, the extension of untruth and deceit, such as introspective method, endogenous method, Self-formation analysis, and regression hypnotherapy. It brings up the past life unpleasant feelings which are already preserved by inscription and deleted. Those methods only invite the dependence of responsibility and the shifting of responsibility, and there is no meaning or significance. As a result, people who use those methods are not able to control their consciousness and get muddled, and in fact, many of them suffer Kundalini syndrome or schizophrenic type mental disorders.

People who live the way of PARAREVO understand that making the consciousness feedback to the past does not have any meaning or significance. It is because in the rule of cosmological causality, we are the ones choosing our own parents based on Self-determination in the past life and in the present life, and we direct our life by the scenario we had drawn by ourselves. Therefore, we shoulder the role and the responsibility to complete spiritual evolution by ourselves, by accomplishing Self-responsibility to *accept all the scenarios based on Self-determination as they are, unconditionally and totally.*

The PARAREVO people understand that memories of the past are useless for living in the present, so they make the Self-effort to avoid expressing emotion or empathy toward the past and the future. They comprehend the fundamental truth of the universe which is

Chapter Four ☆ The Conclusion

how they live in the Now, significantly, valuably, and existentially.

I believe that many psychics and fortune tellers, also psychologists, hypnotherapists, psychotherapists, and counselors who bring out the past and the future of person's life and intervene with the personality and the spirituality without any caution, are the symbolic presence of the demon's world which misleads the life of people. Moreover, people who are saying that they are the reincarnation of Buddha or the Second Coming of Jesus are the fraudsters, who are very persuasive, developed in cunning and guile, and lie unconcernedly. They are well aware of the weak points of the human mind, and have cunning knowledge to drive a person into Self-trapping by anxiety and fear, control them by conducting their dependence on gurus and religions. They pretend as if they have love and are a person of character, but, gradually, deprive the right for existence in life and freedom with anxiety and fear, by bringing up doctrines and fake stories to gain sympathy and impression. They would tell you, that you were a princess in a past life, or a lord, a priest, or a soldier, etc. They would say deceitful things not relative in this life, and get into the person's mind, control the consciousness and brainwash them.

No matter what your past lives were, basically, they have no connection to living in *the Now*. Even though you were a princess or a lord in your past, right now you are exactly what you are. We only need to shoulder Self-responsibility to accept the current position of this life unconditionally and totally, and make Self-completion no matter what others say. Moreover, when we talk about past lives, nobody knows exactly what kind of past life in which era. When we follow past life, we have to go back through the history of 3.8

billion years. After following the process of various life evolutions, no matter what past lives or what ancestors we had, we only end up as one bacterium, which is a primitive life entity.

In the meantime, since we have gone through the history of all kinds of life evolutions, there is no meaning at all in discussing a past life somewhere in one particular past generation. As a result, you would not obtain anything, but only lose your precious freedom time. So if you are concerned about your past lives, your consciousness becomes muddled by the unimportant past, spoils the most important present time, and makes it difficult to live in the Now.

Here is a conclusion. The Logos to release the direct subconscious is "Dear SHINSEI, as you accept me unconditionally, I accepted the facts of entire past lives related to me. Thank you." It is nothing more than that and nothing less than that.

4-21. Emerging consciousness is the final chapter of spiritual evolution

I will explain the most important concept in order to *live in the "Now."* First, we have to release the trash in the consciousness which is sorrow and ONSHU of the past, by love, and not bring them to the present.

The formation process of the consciousness starts from the instinctive survival consciousnesses as the original existing consciousnesses, and has been built continuously from the subconscious to the instinctive remaining consciousness as the emerging consciousness in the historical process of the eternal life

Chapter Four ☆ The Conclusion

evolution. Memories of the past are always preserved by inscription and re-written to newer and higher information, so that nobody lives a life by bringing the memories of the past over to the present. Therefore, releasing the original existence consciousness, releasing the subconscious, and ultimately releasing the emerging consciousness will be the supreme way of living a life in the "Now." This is because *the emerging consciousness is located in the final chapter of the spiritual evolution.* So, what kind of life is the supreme way of living in the "Now"?

Releasing the emerging consciousness means to release the ONSHU relationship with the most influential existence in your personality formation history. That existence is the parents. One of the most important truths is this. *The parents do not have a right to choose the children. However, children are born to the parents they choose.* If the parents are able to choose the children, they naturally want to have the ones who are in excellent health both physically and mentally, and have a wonderful personality. And if it is possible to choose that kind of children, the paradise on the earth would have already been established by excellent people who are in the higher spiritual dimension.

It is because *the rule and the definition of physical causality based on retribution, which is considered the fundamental theory of religions based on the earth logical evidence, would be overruled from the beginning, making it possible to release from the curse of religion by the PARAREVO theory which converts the theory of causality to the theory of paradox based on the cosmological evidence.*

The thought of parent-child relations based on the physical

dominating structure, which is the instinctive remaining consciousness resulting from the genetic domination in this world, is that *the parent is the cause and the child is born as a result. This is correct as long as you are considering only the physical body.* However, considering the soul, the spiritual consciousness entity, the children are supposed to be born in order to achieve Self-completion of the role and the responsibility of this world. So they make Self-determination of the life and the parents, and accomplish Self-responsibility for spiritual evolution, which is to accept everything that might happen in life, unconditionally and totally, with gratitude and happiness.

Between the body and the soul, the purpose and motivation based on the cause of origin are developed completely opposite based on the theory of paradox between the rule of "spirit is subjective and body is objective," and the rule of "body is subjective and spirit is objective." The rule of cosmological causality is based on the rule of "spirit is subjective and body is objective." The cause and the subject are the spiritual relationship between child and parents, and the physical relationship between parents and child are the effect and the object, based on the rule of the fundamental causality of life. Therefore, the rule of cosmological causality is the cause by the spiritual consciousness entity of a child, and as a result, the child chooses the gene of a fertilized egg of the physical parents. For example, the spiritual consciousness entity, which has strong material desire, and domination desire, such as status and reputation, will descend again by choosing similar lineage and genes, relatively, based on the rule of "spirit is subjective and body is objective."

Chapter Four ☆ The Conclusion

Since the soul can rule the body, but the body cannot rule the soul, the rule of reincarnation in the cosmological theory is based on the rule of "spirit is subjective and body is objective," and the rule of physical causality in the earth logical theory is based on the rule of "body is subjective and spirit is objective."

The spiritual consciousness entity is undoubtedly freer than the body, and exists in the higher dimension, and holds the cause and subjectivity. As a phenomenon in the natural science world, the things positioned in a higher dimension are possible to fall to the position in a lower dimension without any conditions. However, it is impossible to ascend to a higher dimension from a lower dimension without some kind of power and action of energy. For example, the temperature of hot water goes down to a lower degree without any qualification. However, it is impossible to raise the temperature of cold water to hot water without some kind of energy. This natural rule is called the rule of entropy. Therefore, we must ascend the spiritual dimension to a higher dimension by our Self-effort, and achieve spiritual evolution. Otherwise, there would be no shifting from a lower dimension to a higher dimension.

It is possible to prepare the physical body of the child by parents even if artificial insemination is used, but it is absolutely impossible for human beings to put a soul into a fertilized egg even with artificial insemination, unless a soul itself selects a fertilized egg and descends. Surrogate birth by in-vitro fertilization is getting popular now days, however, it is an idea only from physical point of view, which is based on the rule of "body is subjective and spirit is objective."

The prenatal life is the important period to form the core of love of the personality by being fostered by mother's love and form the back born of the spiritual consciousness entity for life in this world. Therefore, a child born by surrogate birth inherits the genes of the parents for appearances of the body, but for essential content of the soul, a child inherits the sentiment and the mind and the spirit of the surrogate mother, by the rule of the change by birth and re-birth. I would say it will be born as a "gilded child." Since non-PAREVO people do not understand the rule of "soul is subjective and body is objective," which is the fundamental rule of the universe, ignorant parents and medical science do such things illogically and randomly.

4-22. View of life in the universe and on the earth is paradoxical theory and rule

According to the theoretical framework based on the earth logical evidence, the physical body from the parents and the soul from the child appear with time lag in the time axis, so the soul and the body of the life entity on the earth star do not appear as one, synchronically and simultaneously.

Since the rule of the universe is systematized and exists by the principle of dimensional integration based on free love, *things in a lower dimension are always embraced by things in a higher dimension, and things in a higher dimension try to approach things in a lower dimension and direct them to a higher level and try to integrate them.* Therefore, in the rule of the universe, the spiritual nature world is the subject and the material world is integrated as the object, and all things appear and disappear synchronically and

Chapter Four ☆ The Conclusion

simultaneously according to the rule of entropy relativity and the principle of dimensional integration. The information in the higher level is converted digitally every moment, and forced to exist by the rule of preservation by inscription.

However, since the rule of the earth star exists by the principle of dimensional domination, *things in a higher dimension are always dominated by things in a lower dimension, and things in a lower dimension restrict things in a higher dimension and try to approach and direct them to inconvenience and try to dominate them.* The beginning of the life entity on the earth star starts at the moment when an ovum receives a sperm and the spiritual consciousness entity of the soul descends by conception, and then the fertilized egg shines and makes bioluminescence as a life entity in this world. For the rule of the earth, *it makes clear the fact that time difference occurs obviously, and the fact that the material fertilized egg is first and the soul descend later by conception. This proves that it is directed to the rule of "body is subjective and spirit is objective.*

It is proven medically that bioluminescence occurs immediately after the conception descent, but it is not yet understood by modern medical science, why a fertilized egg shines right after insemination.

Like this, the mechanism of the life entity on the earth star is the physical domination structure in which the higher dimension of the soul is dominated by the lower dimension of the body, according to the principle of dimensional domination based on the rule of "body is subjective and spirit is objective." So, the lives on the earth have the fate which is systematized from birth.

4-23. The mechanism of birth of lives born on the earth

All life entities born on the earth have the same mechanism, even the simplest primitive life entity. By corresponding to the change in the earth environment, the relative structure of amino acids and DNA was created, and when the physical environment was set, the soul, the spiritual consciousness entity, descended by conception by the fluctuation of the universe, and bacteria as the primitive life entity was born.

The rule of the universe is carried through the principle of dimensional integration based on the rule of "spirit is subjective and body is objective," *so it is impossible for the higher dimension of the soul to come into existence from the lower material dimension. The life entity called bacteria was not born on the earth unless the soul, as the relative subjectivity, and the material, as the relative objectivity, appeared simultaneously and synchronically according to the rule of entropy relativity.*

The mechanism of the birth of lives born on the earth is explained as follows. *Some kind of malfunction, such as the giant impact when Mars collided with the earth, happened in the slight fluctuation of imperfection in the infinite universe, causing a huge fluctuation. As a result, an enormous crack between the spiritual world in the universe and the material world opened by the rule of entropy relativity. The spiritual consciousness entity of the universe and the materials of the relative structure between amino acids and DNA connected relatively, synchronically and simultaneously, based on the relative wave in the spiritual dimension and the rule of the relative original power, and the life entity was born according*

Chapter Four ☆ The Conclusion

to the spiritual dimension.

Since the universe forms the harmony and the order and creates the sustainable power and energy by the relative original power which occurs or derives by the mechanism of the slight fluctuation of imperfection of the relative things based on the rule of entropy relativity, when the balance was lost, causing a big fluctuation and crack between the spiritual world and the material world, lower animals carrying the body were born on the earth, an extremely rare phenomenon in the universe. The earth environment changed dramatically after the giant impact. The biggest changes were the emergence of the moon and of water.

4-24. The relative relationship between the physical body and the soul

Spiritual disorders happen as a phenomenon in case the descended soul was spiritually weak and had little power, and the person born in such a condition might suffer from schizophrenia type delusions and auditory hallucinations, severe schizophrenia itself, or multiple personality disorder. Because, in those examples, several souls are compounded in one physical body, so the consciousness grows dim and distracted, by being relative.

The sexual deviation disorder, such as gender identity disorder, is a good example to explain this theory. Gender identity disorder is a phenomenon in which even if the body is a man, the soul, which conducts the mind, is a woman, or vice versa, when the body is a woman the soul is a man. So, as a result, they are attracted to the same genders physically and emotionally, and are known as homosexual. This fact shows clearly that the soul and the physical body were not born from the same unit, but the soul descended by conception from another dimension at the moment when the fertilized egg was prepared and matched with it, and the spirit and the body were integrated. The case of gender identity disorder might be either the mismatch of the spirit and the body, or it was done by the Self-determination of the soul by wishing to have such an experience. From the point of the rule of the universe, I think the latter seems more appropriate. The reason for such a peculiar presence of the life form in which "body is subjective and spirit is objective" is because the earth is the prison star.

Also, there is another explanation why the soul is more cause and subjective than the body. The impulse of sentiment and spirit of those who have gender identity disorder is not caused by the physical side, but the subjectivity and cause exist in the soul. Because, for instance, a person whose body is a man but the soul is a woman often wishes to change the body to woman to agree with the soul, but never directs the soul to agree with the body, and a person whose body is a woman but the soul is a man often directs the soul and wishes to change the body to man. Thus, the subjectivity and the cause are contained in the soul, and the body is always directed to be comprehended to the soul, and the soul always tries to integrate with the body.

So, the body has always had a possibility to be integrated to the soul and it becomes the object and the result, according to the principle of dimensional integration based on the rule of "soul is subjective and body is objective," and the physical evolution has been directed to the way the spiritual consciousness entity wished. As a result, in the history of the physical evolution of human beings, our physical body has become the shape and form of the present human body by that accomplishment, because our spiritual consciousness entity wished to do so. If we had continued to be dominated by the instinctive survival consciousnesses, according to the rule of "body is subjective and soul is objective," the process called evolution would never exist.

The fundamental mistake of the theory of causality in the Buddhist doctrines is, the cause has been limited by the past physical presence such as parents and ancestors, and has continued to be dominated physically and dominated by physical world values and ideas, which are the instinctive remaining consciousnesses, by the genetic domination. However, since history exists on the fact which has been achieved, evolution toward the higher level and positive way by the rule of "spirit is subjective and body is objective," nobody denies the fact that in the present time, all civilization and society is in a much higher stage of dimension than the past.

The fundamental rule of the universe is *the presence which is being relative by the relative original power based on freedom and love, so that the vector of the universe always works for things in a lower dimension to be comprehended to things in a higher dimension, and things in a higher dimension try to integrate things in a lower dimension by directing to a higher level.* It has been proved, as the earth logical fact that our evolution has been brought about, by constantly forming the harmony and the order of the higher level based on the cosmological truth.

4-25. The rule of causality and the rule of karma will collapse

The rule of causality and the rule of karma are the theoretical framework and the common sense on the earth star, in which the cause and the subjectivity exist in the time axis of ancestors and past lives. However, the rule of causality and the rule of karma are the lack of common sense in the universe. Since the future is created by the past existing in the relative position, it can be called the virtual world, so like being caught by the past, being caught by the future is also meaningless and insignificant.

The cause of the life entity of this world is not the physical parents, but exists in the soul of a child who is in the forefront of history. The mechanism and the system in the universe are always inserted for new people and new era, and are led by Self-determination and Self-responsibility based on the rule of freedom. The spiritual evolution is directed that way, so it is possible for everybody to accomplish Self-completion equally in this world, right now, by the rule of preservation by inscription.

If the parents have the responsibility but not the children, the responsibility of the spiritual evolution derives from the parents, which is in the past presence, so it means that the history recedes to the past and there would be no process called evolution. Since the responsibility for evolution is entrusted to the children, we are able to sustain the generation and the development and achieve spiritual evolution to a higher dimension, so, as the saying goes, "listen to your children when you are old." If we always shift responsibility to parents or others, and give up taking our responsibility by ourselves, we will be not able to achieve Self-completion to acquire freedom, and we will lose the possibility for spiritual evolution to a new page of history. Thus, we all have a responsibility to be independent for freedom, so the rule of reincarnation continues until we integrate to the trinity of independence, responsibility, and freedom, and achieve Self-completion. This is the fundamental truth of the universe and the rule to acquire real freedom, which is not to depend on anything and not be dominated by anything.

The rule of causality of retribution, which has been considered the established theory of the religions doctrines, is the theory of the material world centered in the physical domination on the earth star, and it has come from the idea in the chain of the instinctive remaining consciousnesses by the physical genetic domination, and has been defined by the theory produced from the illogical thought of parent-child. The PARAREVO theory knocks the bottom out of those established theories so deceiving the society and people by making them shift responsibility to the parents or others by false and fake theories will be impossible.

Since parents are the ones who prepared the physical body for the child, they have a role and responsibility to deliver and raise their children well in order for them to survive in this world. However, the most important assignment for the parents for their own personality formation, is to complete the role and responsibility to manifest as an ideal married couple of love, by loving each other, nurturing each other and, understanding each other, being a role model for the personality formation of their children.

In order to become *real* parents, they should both shoulder Self-responsibility to show their children the existing purpose and the existing value of life through practices of love, rather than words.

To keep their children from becoming excessively dependent, parents must constantly guide and educate them of the fact that the role and responsibility for independence in order to acquire true freedom, are up to the children themselves, based on the principle of Self-responsibility.

But if people continue to try to escape from themselves, marriage, and family by succumbing to victim consciousness and depending on religious groups as a cover, shifting responsibility to parents and others for their convenience, and giving up Self-responsibility, it is insensitive and a betrayal toward parents, family, and others. Those who depend on religions prove that they had not released the sorrow and ONSHU by the principle of Self-responsibility, so they are not facing seriously the sorrow and the core of ONSHU toward their parents, which is connoted in them, and at the same time, they reveal the lowness of their spiritual dimension. It means they are affirming by themselves that *I depend on religions because I have a grudge against my parents and others,* but all causes, problems and assignments are contained and exist in themselves.

The universe is based on the principle of equality, and all results prove that *all things are based on the rule of freedom, and led by Self-management by Self-determination and Self-completion by Self-responsibility. Therefore, they are equal.* All things happening in this world are our own assignments and responsibility, so there is no cause or problem in the parents or others. If we continue to depend on religions, fortune-telling, past life therapy, hypnotherapy, etc., directing ourselves to Self-escape and shifting responsibility by victim consciousness, it would become a Self-injurious behavior which is equal to great sin and invite Self-destruction, building a chain of misfortune.

It is said that brainwashing by religions is frightening, however, the more frightening thing is the fact that the person connotes the poor and ugly ONSHU inside him/herself toward the parents, family or others, and have an inferior and poor heart, because the personality dimension of the person is low, so the cause and problem is merely the low spiritual dimension of the person. Those kinds of people are nursing each other's wounds in the same spiritual dimension, according to the rule of the relative original power and the rule of gathering by the power of consciousness, and enjoy criticizing others and other religions. The believers who are in the "Astral lower spiritual dimension" tend to gather in religious groups in the "Astral lower spiritual dimension."

People who are in a higher spiritual dimension never involve themselves in religion from the beginning, and never fall into the dependence of religion. When those who belong to religious groups learn the PARAREVO theory, they would say that "it is the same as our religion." This proves that their understanding is in the lower spiritual dimension and they are not capable of understanding the difference, just like ants see all stones as the same even though one might be Mt. Fuji or Mt. Everest.

4-26. Spiritual evolution and the "exclusion theory by jealousy" are opposites

The truth of the universe based on the PARAREVO theory is the paradoxical theory from religions or established philosophical theories on the earth.

Since you have selected your parents by yourself according to the scenario of life, which you had programmed for spiritual evolution, the release of the emerging consciousness is "father and mother, thank you for bringing me to this world." It is not more than that and not less than that. It is important that only gratitude exists toward the parents without any demand or dependence.

Many people who use methods like success philosophy or Self-development, such as introspective method, endogenous method, and degenerative hypnotherapy, invite the disturbance of the consciousness, and delve into the personality formation history to bring up the memories of the past which are already preserved by inscription and deleted deliberately. People who use those methods often have lost mental integrity and are not able to be socially independent. Many people who have grudge and hard feelings against their parents by considering them as the object for Self-evaluation, take those methods and spend lots of money, and eventually end up with a schizophrenia type mental disorder. *Parents are not the objects of the Self-evaluation, but are the assignment testing us to see how much we accept sorrow and ONSHU against them with love, gratitude and happiness and establish Self-integration in the "Now."*

It is because the rule of universe considers and arranges based on the equation that *we should place the lovable ONSHU as the closest presence, and by loving that ONSHU we can release our own ONSHU. We made Self-determination to reincarnate in this world for Self-completion to release the blind spot of the Mobius loop of vertical love* and the blind spot of the Mobius loop of *horizontal love,* which are the parent-child relationship, the brother-sister

Chapter Four ☆ The Conclusion

relationship, and husband-wife relationship as the pivot point of necessity for the assignment of responsibility of life.

However, *the rule of exclusion theory by jealousy* is the totally opposite theory, which is *to lose the things you love and lose your position by excluding and expelling the ONSHU by jealousy*. For example, there is trouble between wife and mother-in-law and father-in law. In the rule of the universe, it is a natural role and responsibility for them to love their son's wife more than they love their own son, because they receive a daughter from outside the family who has grown with loving care by her parents. However, they foolishly fall victim to jealousy because their son's wife took their lovely son from them, and start treating her badly and openly speak ill of her to others, according to the rule of the exclusion theory by jealousy. They increase the relative original power with unpleasant feelings with many people, and create the demon world by amplifying unpleasant emotions in themselves. And, as a result, they often lose the fortune and even the life of their loving son, narrow their own place, or quite often happen to fall into unpleasant feelings, or unavoidably become ill and shorten their own life. They invite further ONSHU, have a tendency to change their personality to ugly, and finally invite Self-destruction. So, we can say that *the rule of exclusion theory by jealousy is the root of all evil in human society.*

We must understand and be prepared to accept the fact that all human relations in life are based on this rule. People, to whom you relate in all communities, such as in a family, a school, a company and a society, are the assignment for your own spiritual evolution, and you should understand that they are an irreplaceable, essential and precious personal fortune.

Therefore, you should not exercise the rule of exclusion theory by jealousy, but complete your life with great virtue of unselfishness by Self-sacrifice.

4-27. Logos to release emerging consciousness

The ONSHU and sorrow hidden in the personality formation history would never be released by religion dependence or groups of the mental world. They will add the ONSHU by the time axis domination and become the cause of Self-injurious behavior resulting in loss of coordination disorder, as the opposite effect. So since they are not necessary for your life, you should never involve them. The stronger you have ONSHU in the parent-child relationship or husband-wife relationship, the more you are trapped by religion dependence or groups of the mental world.

We should not direct the consciousness to the past and the future, but should live in the "Now" meaningfully, valuably and existentially. Since the only purpose in this material world is a preparation period for the spiritual life in the spiritual world of the universe (Cosmic world) the fastest way to ensure Self-realization is to complete the steps of the actual circumstances of the present with gratitude and happiness, step by step, existentially with Self-effort and Self-responsibility.

So, *we should live only in the "Now" in this world, should live the "Now" of death and live the "Now" of after death.* In the after death world, there is no past or future, so there is no other way but to live existentially. *To live in the "Now" is the way of life to integrate the*

Chapter Four ☆ The Conclusion

entire universe from the tangible substantial world to the intangible substantial world. The Logos to release the emerging consciousness is "Dear SHINSEI, as you accept me unconditionally, I accepted my parents and the assignment responsibility of life unconditionally. Thank you."

4-28. Logos to live in the "Now"

When we transcend the accumulated consciousnesses of the past which are the original existence consciousness, the subconscious, and the emerging consciousness, and digitalize them to the zero time period of each moment, the "Now," face SHINSEI, and accept as they are unconditionally and totally with gratitude and happiness, we have the most fundamental and core of the way of life of PARAREVO.

Those accumulated entities of the consciousnesses are all like the ghost of the past. Only the "Now" is the integrated moment of the past by the rule of preservation by inscription. So there exists just the truth, that we are lived by the "rule of attainment of the spiritual being during life" by the relative original power between SHINSEI, which is the integrated verity of the individual entity, and the spiritual consciousness entity, which is the individual mental entity. And the fact, which we live the "Now" existentially, for the spiritual evolution by the relative original power between the spiritual consciousness entity and the body.

Therefore, the "Now," which represents the entire history, is set in the forefront of the life entity, and it is the only moment to be integrated in the whole universe. Here are the Logos to live in the

"Now." "Dear SHINSEI, because of the truth that I am lived in the "Now" by you, I am going to live to complete the "Now" as the fact. Thank you." It is the way of life to persist in the undeniable existentialism, and the role and the responsibility for Self-completion to go the intangible substantial world after spiritual evolution.

4-29. Separation of "I" is the true way of life

To draw the separation borderline between oneself "I" and others will be the most important concept in order to live the irreplaceable and precious life, as "I" am the leading actor of my own life. The separation borderline of oneself and others is the borderline whether "I" is the subject or the object, and whether it is the cause or the effect. Your life would be significantly different whether you can draw the dividing line between you and all objects, including your own body, or not. This dividing line is more important than the border between nations, because we should make the subject word "I" clearly in order to shoulder Self-responsibility without shifting the responsibility of the assignment of your life.

Also the importance of this borderline is that it establishes the policy and the concept to clarify Self-management by Self-determination and Self-completion by Self-responsibility toward one's life. This borderline will determine the important turning point to complete the assignment responsibility of one's life. We sometimes make a great mistake in choosing our life, like "putting the cart before the horse," because we may be not able to draw this borderline between others and ourselves by our misjudging the insignificant for the essential.

Chapter Four ☆ The Conclusion

We sometimes reverse the importance by emitting the emotion carelessly toward the relative object and phenomenon called fact, which means that we empathize to the condition and phenomenon as if it is the subject and cause, and get unpleasant feelings by ourselves as the object, and we spoil our own feelings with Self-hatred such as complaints, dissatisfaction, jealousy, anxiety, fear, anger, and hard feelings and those feelings will become our truth.

Since we have been tamed, throughout history, by the acquisition competition for others evaluation under the evil competition principle, it becomes difficult to distinguish the borderline between Self-evaluation and others evaluation, and almost impossible to draw the separation borderline between others and ourselves. For instance, as I mentioned before, the author from Japan who won the Novel Prize for literature, committed suicide, even though he obtained worldwide evaluation from others, he invited the worst conclusion of Self-injurious behavior and took his own life.

We have to draw this borderline by distinguishing fact and truth. Truth is the existence of SHINSEI, which is the consciousness based on SHINSEI, and fact is the existence of things, which is the phenomenon based on things. All things existing outside of the consciousness, including your own body are fact. Natural environment, family environment, social environment, status, honor, property, the Bible and the Buddhist sutra, all exist as fact of phenomena based on things.

Truth exists in the inner consciousness based on our spiritual dimension. In our consciousness, the "soul mind" and the "body mind," which are relative by SHINSEI based on the rule of entropy relativity, exist in the slight fluctuation of imperfection, synchronically and simultaneously, according to the spiritual dimension. It is totally dependent on truth based on the free intention of the person, whether they evoke the "soul mind" or whether they evoke the "body mind" based on SHINSEI. Even if all people in the world evaluate a person according to the fact that he is an unhappy, if he lives every day with gratitude and happiness, there is no unhappiness anywhere, because happiness as truth exists in the person.

Another example, suppose there is fact that a person was judged wrongly as a criminal by a false charge. If he evoked "body mind" based on SHINSEI, and cursed everybody around him and lived his life with grudge and hard feelings, saying "how could you judge me wrongly even though I am innocent," and made his own spirit and mind like that of a demon, his soul has no choice but goes to the spiritual world filled with bitterness.

Since people who live the way of life of PARAREVO try to complete their way of life of truth which to never shift responsibility or fall into victim consciousness, but accept fact unconditionally and totally with gratitude and happiness. They would say "it is not somebody else's responsibility, because the cause, the problem and the assignment to be judged by the false charge are contained in my soul in past lives," and evoke the "soul mind" based on SHINSEI, and directing to a higher spiritual dimension, they will go to the spiritual world filled with gratitude and happiness as a result, even if they are sentenced to death.

One more example; suppose it is fact that a person was diagnosed with an incurable disease and was informed by a doctor that his remaining time was only two months. If he evoked the poor "body

Chapter Four ☆ The Conclusion

mind" based on SHINSEI, saying "why me? Did I receive hate from somebody? Did I eat some kind of carcinogenic substance?" The truth is he made his consciousness ill by making himself sick by falling into victim consciousness, shifting responsibility with grievance, cursing the illness and his life with anxiety and fear toward the death of the body, and he will go to the spiritual world where there are only sick souls with anxiety and fear.

People who live the way of PARAREVO know that they will go to the spiritual world where there are only healthy souls, with gratitude and happiness as a result even if they are informed that they are dying. They would not make their mind suffer and would achieve health for their consciousness, by evoking noble "soul mind" based on SHINSEI and accept the fact unconditionally and totally with gratitude and happiness, saying "thank you for giving me a difficult task," because it will become their truth, no matter what the fact is.

In the PARAREVO theory, the existing purpose and the existing value for life is Self-Enlightenment and spiritual evolution in order to go to the spiritual world of the universe, so the biggest assignment responsibility and theme are how much we could build *the achievement of truth for a higher spiritual dimension* in this life. The PARAREVO theory pays the greatest attention and Self-effort to distinguish fact based on the rule of "body is subjective and spirit is objective," and truth based on the rule of "spirit is subjective and body is objective," toward all phenomena which might happen, and always direct oneself to a higher spiritual dimension.

This is *the fundamental difference between the way of life of the Jesus type in the lower spiritual dimension, in which fact was tossed around and lost truth, and the way of life of PARAREVO in the higher spiritual dimension, which oversees fact and completes truth to a higher level.* It is because truth exists in the spiritual dimension of each person, and in the spiritual world *there is no fact better than truth.*

4-30. Separation borderline between love and kindness

The difficult choice in drawing the separation borderline between oneself and others is drawing the line *between love and kindness.* If you violate this borderline by mistake, you may *misunderstand love for kindness, and it could cause big trouble in your life.*

Since the existing purpose and the existing value for our life is Self-Enlightenment and spiritual evolution, there are many difficult situations and circumstances we may encounter in our life. But, please remember that the best equation to direct to Self-Enlightenment and spiritual evolution is *to complete the responsibility to be independent and acquire freedom.*

All facts happen in this life are the result of the assignment of the responsibility that you had selected for spiritual evolution based on truth, such as being ill, being reduced to poverty, or being born in a poor family environment. There are no assignments for Self-Enlightenment and spiritual evolution which you are not able to overcome by yourself. Because you had decided in the spiritual world, by Self-responsibility, and acquired the confidence to accomplish Self-completion for the assignments without fail, you descended again to this life.

Chapter Four ☆ The Conclusion

Giving a hand to help a troubled person or lending money is kindness but not love. Real love is to direct the person toward acquiring freedom by taking the responsible act in order to be independent, and keeping an eye on that person. Troubled situations are the assignments for a person to achieve Self-Enlightenment and spiritual evolution. The person must overcome the facts by Self-effort and be independent by the principle of Self-responsibility, which is the truth that the person himself has to shoulder. We should not take this opportunity for Self-Enlightenment away from the person with our kindness.

The definitions of kindness and love based on the PARAREVO theory are as follows. *Kindness is hypocrisy by Self-satisfaction and directs to the principle of dependence and domination. On the other hand, love is deep affection by Self-sacrifice and directs to the principle of independence and freedom.*

Young persons, who have been raised with overprotection and over-interference by the kindness of ignorant parents, are not able to be independent, even at home, and some of them fall victim to domestic violence by shutting themselves in. The reason those youths are not able to be independent, and instead choose an easy life such as NEET (not in education, employment or training) or permanently job-hopping being only part-time workers, is because of ignorant and foolish parents who are not able to draw the separation borderline between love and kindness. They have confused love and kindness, and give kindness but not real love to their children. This is called *"parasite syndrome."*

Love raises people but kindness spoils people. So, the economically wealthy nations are more likely to have the parasite syndrome (dependence syndrome- people who are not able to be independent socially).

Children who have been raised with overprotection and over-interference are exactly the same as the animals in the zoo which have been raised by humans and are not able to go back to their natural environment. The cause of a habit of mind which is not able to draw the separation borderline between oneself and others gets into a habit resulting from the history of personality formation based on the rule of the wrong causality in the causal relationship between the parents and the child.

4-31. Only truth exists in the spiritual world

We were born to this life according to the rule of reincarnation, after determining in the spiritual world, our own assignments for this world. The spiritual consciousness entity exists based on the "rule of the attainment of the spiritual being during life," in the zero time period, the Now, in which the time axis does not exist. The memories of the spiritual consciousness entity were sealed by the physical domination structure at the moment it descended by conception to the fertilized egg, and the new assignments and the old memories appear and are deleted at the same time, according to the rule of preservation by inscription, based on the rule of freedom, and the new life activity in this world begins synchronically and simultaneously.

In order to achieve spiritual evolution in this world, we should make Self-completion for the assignment of responsibility toward life with modesty and humility, which is to *accept all facts which*

Chapter Four ☆ The Conclusion

might happen in this life, and direct them to truth of a higher spiritual dimension, by the presence of the consciousness based on SHINSEI, and accept them unconditionally and totally with gratitude and happiness.

Since the personality formation history in this life will be the compilation and the final chapter of the entire personality formation history in the past lives, we should understand that it is set in the forefront of spiritual evolution. However, in the theoretical framework and value in this world, we tend to live for the effort to increase status and property by acquisition competition for evaluation by others, which we will lose eventually, as a fate, and for pursuit and acquisition of honor by the relative evaluation by irresponsible people. And then we would spend our life seeking the physical world benefits, and live a momentary and empty life which is fact. Therefore, we are not able to obtain the true sense of accomplishment toward life, and not able to achieve the responsibility of assignment. We are also dominated by the personality destruction and the rule of reincarnation, and will repeat again and again the life on the earth star, which is more like only dust in the universe.

The true purpose and the value in this life are not in the physical world benefits but in the spiritual world benefits. We must aim to obtain the value toward *truth of Self-evaluation* based on the spiritual world benefits, by the paradigm not to cross the separation borderline between ourselves and others, according to the truth of internal evaluation and the value (the individual art of love), beyond the external evaluation and the value of the physical world benefits.

We would never understand the existing purpose and the real

value of the earth star if we evaluate and discuss only the earth dimension. Unless we observe and are inspired by the higher dimension of the universe, outside the earth, we are not able to understand the overview of the existing purpose of the earth star, just like we cannot see the forest for the trees.

We take the same conventional ecological action and come and go our own way without distinguishing the consciousness of truth and fact throughout 3.8 billion years of the outdated life form, from bacterium to human beings we live with the common desire consciousness dominated by the instinctive survival consciousnesses. *The Bible, sutra and Buddhist scriptures are only one fact.* Since many religious groups and sects have been born from the truth of the founder of a religion and the originator who touched those based on their spiritual dimension, it proves that *the Bible, sutra and Buddhist scriptures exist as fact, however, there is no truth in there.*

We should draw the separation borderline between our own internal "body mind" and ourselves based on the internal value as the subject, connect the relative wave with the "soul mind" based on each spiritual dimension and SHINSEI, create the relative original power, exercise the real nature consciousness, and then make Self-effort for Self-creation and Self-completion to achieve Self-evaluation to a higher spiritual dimension, by conducting acts to complete to happiness based on the motivation of love. It is because *there is no fact existing over truth,* so based on the rule of "spirit is subjective and body is objective," *only truth exists in the spiritual world, and there is no fact based on the physical world benefits, the theory of good or evil, or the theory of superiority or inferiority.*

4-32. Lose truth being fooled by fact

People in this world always worry about other's evaluation for protection of their own respectability and vanity, and live by spending the majority of the consciousness for that, and make every effort to win the acquisition competition for other's evaluation. We have been directed to the rule of "body is subjective and spirit is objective" from the moment we were born in this world, so all five physical senses are directed to the outside. We have been tamed by those physical senses throughout 3.8 billion years and made the formation of the consciousness. Our eyes and ears are always directed to the outside, so we are constantly directing our interest to the outside. We have communicated with our parents, confirmed love and ONSHU by the words and deeds of the parents, reached the society and the culture, and walked the personality formation history by the external environment.

We are always confirming the evaluation through the five physical senses, have been tamed to evaluate based on superiority or inferiority and good and evil, and on the extension of this idea, confirmed our own behaviors against others' evaluation unconsciously, and determined right or wrong for Self-evaluation, and made the habit of the consciousness by those thoughts. For example, many women wish to become more beautiful and pursue appearances and fashion, and men aim to be good-looking, intelligent, well-educated with high income. Those are all for the purpose of the acquisition competition of the external evaluation toward the opposite sex.

They do not verify and confirm their internal Self-evaluation in order to direct their spiritual dimension to a higher level for personality improvement and spirituality improvement. They could someday fall into Self-hatred and Self-denial, get some kind of mental illness and/or physical illness, and reach to Self-destruction by Self-injurious behavior. Our social structure is made to learn, unconditionally, the habit of the way of life by which we are made fools by the facts and lose the truth, getting priorities backwards. So the fact called external evaluation becomes the subject and truth called the internal evaluation becomes the object.

The concept of each person's life and the paradigm are formed by the environment and the experience, based on each personality formation history, and manifest as the habit of mind of each spiritual dimension. The only purpose to draw the separation borderline between oneself and others is *to shift the habit of mind so as not to be made a fool of by fact but to live in truth, and acquire real freedom.* Even though, as the fact, you live in a miserable environment or have an illness, and have the sympathy of other people, you should draw the separation borderline between you and fact, direct the consciousness to the "soul mind" of the relative subjectivity based on SHINSEI, accept the given environment and illness unconditionally and totally with gratitude and happiness by truth, secure Self-responsibility in order to guarantee the rule of freedom, and make Self-effort to direct to courage and belief.

Even if people acquire physical world benefits such as status, honor and property which people are envious of, as fact, by the acquisition competition for others' evaluation, if they are not able to draw the separation borderline between themselves and others, and not able to have the consciousness of modesty and humility for all things because of arrogant thoughts, they would have unpleasant feelings and fall into a worldly and momentary trap of truth without gratitude and happiness. Ultimately, the soul of those people selects the truth of the inconvenient and poor spiritual world called Self-destruction by the fact of physical domination, holding the worldly attachment and ONSHU, and they decide, by themselves, to be dominated by the rule of inconvenient reincarnation beyond the verge of life and death.

4-33. Separation borderline between self and others in the personality formation history

It is important to make Self-effort to draw the separation borderline between oneself and others toward the habit of mind based on the personality formation history and live and die the life established with Self-integration as the subject of "I," throughout your lifetime.

The personality formation histories are mainly divided by the natural environment, the social environment, the cultural environment, the mind and spirit environment of parent-child, the mind and spirit environment of husband and wife, and the time axis domination. And the greatest influence on the personality formation history is the time axis domination, which has a relation to all experiences.

4-34. Time to face the natural world seriously

To draw the separation borderline between oneself and the natural environment is quite difficult. It is because we are given a life to live by the rule of nature in the natural environment. Our outside environment, including the sun and the moon, air to breathe, water, food, such as fruits and vegetables, and clothing and shelter are not originally created by human beings. This is because our life is blessed by nature and relies on the benefits of nature and we are forced to exist according to the universe and the rule of the natural world. We human beings rein at the top of the food chain, fall into the arrogant idea called the *science almighty principle* without noticing, have the illusion that we are able to dominate even the nature world, and forget gratitude and love and respect to the benefits from nature.

We are no longer able to co-exist or mutually prosper with the natural world. Human beings plunged into the termination era in which each of us should go back to the starting point for the life ethics and try to prepare to face the natural world sincerely. This problem has spread out globally, regardless of ethnic groups, races and nations. Therefore, it is absolutely impossible to solve this problem by the effort of one nation. In recent years, the most threatening natural phenomena globally, are, flood accompanied with global warming, and the desertification phenomenon, in which land became barren after a flood. Those two extreme types of water phenomena of remarkable environmental destruction are spreading on a global scale. Now various counties in the world are not seeking economy, petrochemical energy or food, but water. In fact water

Chapter Four ☆ The Conclusion

is overwhelmingly in shortage. We are on the planet of water, the earth, and still many people in the world are seeking water. Water is in critical shortage, now days.

How did we get into such a situation? Since water plays the role as a guard of the earth star, the prison planet, the PARAREVO theory raises the alarm that we are receiving a counterattack from water, and the bill for desecrating the natural world, because of human arrogance, will come due. We brought on the anger of the spiritual presence which handles water. Therefore, unless we understand the spiritual presence which superintends water, this problem will never be solved. The flood trial in the story of Noah's Ark, in the Old Testament, is not entirely false.

In the whole creator world, which exists in the natural world on the earth, as the individuality being relative to all things, the spiritual presences exist as two sides of the same coin. Water nurtures and works for all living things, and provides food and benefits for them. For example, it is said that bizarre phenomena and unfortunate things happen once wells are buried in the ground without permission. That superstition would not derive groundlessly. Based on experience and fact, it has been handed down through history.

Water carries out creation, destruction, integration, and domination at the same time, toward the environment of lives on the earth star, according to the rule of balance. So, air, wind, and rain, all are created by water, and cause various phenomena, and perform purification and regeneration on a global scale. Therefore, the terrestrial life in Gaia is forced to live by depending on and being given the gift of water.

4-35. The time for judgment by water

The major civilizations in the world are blessed by water. The culture and the civilization have flourished with the center around the great rivers rich with water. Therefore, the nations which respect the great rivers receive the benefits of all things unconditionally, because the river brings wealth and prosperity.

However, there were nations in the world that brought about their own collapse, leaving a terrible stain on history, because of their ignorance. For example, the Aral Sea was the fourth largest lake, which separated Europe and Asia. In 1960, because of the great mistake of the unintelligent cultivation of farmlands of the Soviet Union, water levels began decreasing due to human greedy needs. At the time, Uzbekistan cultivated cotton which used large amounts of irrigation water, and pumped the irrigation water to the desert on a large scale, as if to show that the policy of the Soviet Union succeeded. However, because of sloppy development and cultivation, all water was absorbed into the desert. As a result, the quantity of water in the Aral Sea today is 1,150 square kilometers, which is a decrease in volume of 90 percent, and the surface area has shrunk 73% making it 17,600 square kilometers. The Aral Sea was divided into South Aral Lake and North Aral Lake, and as it dried up, millions of hectares became desertification and it was called the Arakan desert. From this desert, 75 million tons of dust and salt flew in all directions with the wind, forming a sphere which reached to 1,000km radius and accelerated the desertification of the Eurasian continent. Of course, the Soviet Union was forced to Self-destruction by the anger of the spiritual presence of water.

Chapter Four ☆ The Conclusion

On May 20, 2006, due to the completion of the China Yangtze River Three Gorges Dam, a major artery in the nature world was blocked, and due to the myocardial infarction of the natural world in Eastern Asia, it is accelerating worldwide environmental degradation. The countries suffering the most from the damages caused by this dam are Taiwan and Japan. Of course, in the future, in China, desertification will become more serious because of this mistake. Water of the Yangtze River will lose its` direction and flow into cracks in the basement of active faults, big earthquakes will occur everywhere because of the fault slip, and the result may be that the home country will be destroyed.

The construction of the dam blocked the blood vessels of the nature world and has caused so much destruction to the natural environment. Because we do not know the proper treatment of water, it makes the chain of unhappiness by a negative spiral on a global scale, and accelerates and expands on the planet of water.

Now water is a most precious thing. Since Japan is an island country, blessed with water, it is hard to understand the value of water easily, however, the Chinese have already started buying Japanese land and searching for water. Unless we restore the rivers, which are the vessels of the natural world, it is impossible for us to regenerate the nature world.

4-36. Now is the time to receive judgment from water

The soul, our spiritual consciousness entity, is forced to exist inconveniently by the mechanism of the prison planet, according to the physical domination structure by genetic domination. And water is the presence to dominate the life entity on the earth star, more than the physical domination structure. Our soul is connoted in our physical body, and the body is composed of mostly water, so I could say that from bacteria to plants, animals, and human beings, the soul is entirely sealed by water. In other words, it is like wearing clothes of water. Therefore, all life entities are equally under the thumb of water domination.

Suppose the earth is the life entity Gaia. The earth itself is covered and sealed by water, as the physical phenomenon, and wears clothes of water, but, the more important thing is to be aware of the spiritual presence of water. This is because the rule of the universe is carried through the rule of "spirit is subjective and body is objective," so we are directed to spiritual intention, and creation and integrity will be done. The rule of the earth is carried through the rule of "body is subjective and spirit is objective," and is directed to material thoughts, and destruction and domination will be inevitable. Human beings should become spiritually wise and connect spiritually with the whole creator world, sincerely. Otherwise, we may end up selecting the path to Self-destruction, like the former Soviet Union.

Hereafter, *human beings should obtain spiritual intelligence more than brain intelligence.* If we make an error in how we treat water, the guard of the prison planet, it might invite unexpected situations, and cause the purification phenomenon as the rite of passage of water, and the result could be many sacrifices. When we deal with water for excessive physical world benefits, by ignorant desire with no knowledge of the mechanism for life on the prison star, we will not be able to cross even the "River," the borderline of the spiritual world after death, and being Self-trapped, will remain on the earth.

When we listen to the heartrending cry of Gaia and face water, and go into action by considering the effective use of water sincerely, the regeneration of the nature world will be completed rapidly by water, because the earth is the water planet. In the near future, the economic revolution and the environmental revolution will occur by various energies created by water, such as a vehicle run by water and an airplane powered by water. Those energies will all return to water. They are the energies which will not create negative legacies, so the entropy would not increase or decrease and we will be able to create stable energies.

In order for our spiritual consciousness entity to release from the physical body, we should, first of all, release the water domination of the body, then release the genetic domination, release the instinctive remaining consciousness, and finally release the physical dominating structure. So, releasing the dominating structure of water will be the most important concept to release the soul from the body.

By releasing the oxygen dominating structure of water molecules, taking out free energy and releasing the water molecule itself, the spiritual presence of water will be released from water and at the same time, water itself will be able to ascend the dimension, and sublimate. According to that mechanism and equation, *the dominating structure of the entire earth star will be released, the spiritual gravity of space wave becomes lighter, and the spiritual dimension of the earth itself will ascend.* Thus, by the relative original power, the wave of Gaia will ascend, and it is directed to the criterion of the "soul mind" of a higher spiritual dimension, and the path to spiritual evolution will be opened easily.

4-37. Separation borderline between oneself and others in the material world

Since we are the existence of the instinctive survival consciousnesses, as a fate of the earth star, in order for us to survive we have to be materially dependent. At the moment we abandon dietary desire, it means death, and at the moment we abandon sexual desire, we are not able to preserve the species and will become extinct. The terrestrial life is an extremely rare and unusual life entity, a unique life phenomenon in the universe, because of shouldering the physical desire as a fate.

In the universe, life entities exist as numbers of stars, however, since the life entities of the universe exist at the dimension of the spiritual consciousness entity, it is impossible to confirm the truth at the level of the fact which is in the physical visual range. Many astronomers and religious scholars brag that the earth star is the only planet where the intelligent life entity exists. However, since the material world based on fact is not able to transcend the spiritual world based on truth, it only looks that way by the physical visual range. As proof of this, for the terrestrial life, even though the figures and shapes are different from bacterium to human beings, they have the common ecological behaviors by the common desire consciousness, and complete their lifetime by the fact that all theoretical frameworks and values are built by the instinctive survival consciousnesses, and they are tamed in the material

Chapter Four ☆ The Conclusion

dependence and dominated by materials.

We are enslaved by the whole creator world based on fact which is opposite from the spiritual evolution, so in order to reform this way of life we should draw the separation borderline between ourselves and the whole creator world, retrieve the superintendence and subjectivity in true life, and establish Self-integration. Needless to say, the natural environment is the presence of the phenomenon based on things and the presence of the consciousness based on SHINSEI connoted inside us, so it is up to Self-determination and Self-responsibility how we take the fact. So, whether we create unpleasant feelings or gratitude and happiness, is totally up to oneself based on the rule of freedom.

Since the cause and the subjectivity based on truth is inside you, if somebody cursed, spit and threw a punch at you but you didn't possess any feeling of anger inside, you would accept that situation unconditionally and totally and never be angry. Why is that? Because the cause of the feeling called anger does not exist inside of you, so you are not able to get angry even if you want to. If you are full of anger, you will reveal the anger even when someone touches your clothes. Why is that? It is because the cause and the subjectivity of anger is inside you, so that you are not able to manage the feeling of anger and the anger will come out directly.

No matter how others evaluate you, *the only fact is the irresponsibility of others` evaluation.* So, you should shoulder Self-responsibility for *the truth of Self-evaluation.* Whether you determine Self-evaluation for all things with gratitude and happiness, or determine Self-evaluation for all things with unpleasant feelings, they are all entrusted to the rule of freedom called Self-determination, so that you have to follow *the principle of freedom and responsibility* to shoulder the responsibility as the truth of Self-evaluation. *We are equal because we are given the freedom to determine all things by ourselves.*

Whether Jesus died by completing Self-responsibility and transcending the verge of life and death by shouldering the Cross unconditionally and totally with gratitude and happiness with mercy and affection, or whether he died by shifting his responsibility and transcending the verge of life and death by falling into victim consciousness based on the theory of good or evil, creating criminals outside by the external classification holding the ONSHU and pain, it was up to Jesus himself to make Self-determination and shoulder Self-responsibility, according to the rule of freedom.

4-38. The natural environment and truth of separation borderline between oneself and others

All causes and subjectivities of the consciousness exist as truth of the personality formation history and connote in the feelings of oneself, and those never exist in others, in environment, or in phenomenon including one's own physical body. It is because the environment and phenomenon can be a factor or an inducement as a fact, but can never be the cause and the subjectivity as truth. Therefore, by the environment and the experience in the personality formation history based on the corroboration of the Self-formed consciousness of the spiritual dimension, the motivation of the feeling derives, and the cause and the subjectivity for all action will be manifested as truth, whether it is good or bad.

Chapter Four ☆ The Conclusion

So, people who have connoted unpleasant feelings in their consciousness are dissatisfied no matter what they encounter. For example, they are sure to complain and grumble about the weather, whether it rains, or is hot, or cold, or cloudy or sunny. The natural phenomenon is not the issue. The spiritual dimension based on the personality formation history of that person is too low and poor and filled with unpleasant feelings, which originated in the cause. For example, do Eskimo people complain about the cold? Or do people in Tahiti or Fiji complain about the heat? If so, they would have already emigrated to somewhere else, or the ethnic groups themselves would have collapsed and Self-destructed by stress, and would not even exist at that place. They became completely acclimated to the given environment, accepted it as it was unconditionally and totally, and made the Self-effort to try to direct all environments as the truth, to a higher rank of happiness and gratitude.

We should not direct the arrow to the objects such as the environment and the phenomena and conduct unpleasant empathy carelessly. Instead, the most important for us is to always direct the arrow to the consciousness of oneself (the subject and the cause) to the truth, and surpass the facts of the environment and the phenomena by love, and accept everything, unconditionally, and control all things under Self-integration. Since one's life is led to Self-determination based on the rule of freedom which is the subjectivity and the cause, we should draw the separation borderline between ourselves and others throughout our lifetime, and establish the true life style based on Self-integration, directing the arrow to ourselves. Then we are able to make Self-creation as nice and stylish individual art without pretense.

The secret to receiving invisible support and encouragement from the natural world by getting along with the natural environment is to distinguish between fact and truth. We must recognize that human beings are *the greediest and the most dangerous creatures* among the terrestrial life, and deal with all creatures sincerely with humility and modest feelings. Since human beings rein at the top of the food chain, we do not understand the pain of the nature world, like somebody stepping on another's foot does not understand the pain of the person whose foot was stepped on, so we fell into arrogance without noticing and became the most egoistical and foolish creatures among the terrestrial life.

We slaughter all kinds of animals and plants, exploiting the natural world, and eat them up without any appreciation, and saying it is gourmet. Since all things have a life, we should not forget the feeling of gratitude when we take the life itself, and should connect with them from our heart, in order not to receive reprimand from the whole creator world. The foolishness of human beings is that we are not showing gratitude at all for things which are natural. There are many people who would jump for joy if they were told they were to be given money, however, unfortunately they would never have feelings of gratitude or even have consciousness toward the sun, the moon, or air and water, which have existed naturally since before they were born.

The greatest ignorance of human beings is *we do not distinguish between truth, which is based on "spirit is subjective and body is objective," and fact, which is based on "body is subjective and spirit is objective."* Since the universe is forced to exist by the rule of "spirit is subjective and body is objective," there is no existence which has

Chapter Four ☆ The Conclusion

no consciousness, in the universe. It is because the consciousness directs to complete the existing purpose and the existing value. All things in the whole creator world on the earth star have a consciousness as well. Suppose you are food, what would you feel if you were eaten by somebody who was complaining with unpleasant feelings such as discontent and dissatisfaction? Probably you would think you do not want to be eaten by this kind of person, even though you sacrificed your life for that person. On the other hand, if a person ate you with deepest gratitude and joy from his heart, what would you feel? Probably you would think you were glad to be eaten by this person. This is the spiritual world and since all things are spiritual creatures, the path is opened by feelings. The rule of the universe based on love opens the path of feelings always, and directs to happiness of the higher dimension.

Because of our ignorance we do not understand that the things which do not speak words have been given more rights to reprimand in the spiritual world. Here is the reason for the saying that *ignorance is a shadow of death, does not produce any emotion, and is only alive on the outside but actually is dead on the inside.* If you were in the opposite position and somebody complained all the time, would you like to be close to such a person? You probably would prefer to make distance and try to not be involved with that person.

The symbol of all creation in the human society is money. Since possessing more money than is necessary is the same as making all creation inconvenient without any meaning, we should try to return money to the society, and circulate it freely, without holding the concept of possession. For this reason, it is said that *it is more difficult for the rich to enter heaven than it is for a camel to pass through the eye of a needle.* Those who have attained wealth and are attached to fortune would go to the world in which there is nothing but a mountain of rubble, after their death.

The only thing which can transcend the separation borderline, it is *love of SHINSEI unity.* If you have any emotion or empathy without love of SHINSEI unity you will be mistaking the insignificant for the essential, which confuses the subjectivity and the cause with the objectivity and the effect, and you will inevitably fall into unpleasant feelings.

4-39. The personality formation history based on the social environment and the view of values

As a constituent member of the society, we should respect each individual's dignity and accept each other as the molecules of the individual mental entity connecting with the verge of the individual entity, SHINSEI as the common denominator. This means, even though we are all different as individuals, we can connect with each other because we all have SHINSEI in ourselves, in common. It also means to create and share the happiness of the higher spiritual dimension while expressing the social role and responsibility as the individual art. Doing so by directing the harmony and the order of the whole society to a higher dimension, each person is shouldering the role and the responsibility in order to build the true collaboration society.

However, looking back on the history of spirituality formation, the social environments have been built by the value and environment of each era. For example, the social environment and value in the Edo period in Japan, which had the distinction of rank, and the free social environment and value like modern time, are significantly different. It must have been extremely difficult to draw the separation borderline between oneself and the social environment and value in the era of feudal society accompanied with compelling power, however, discrimination systems exist all over the world even in modern society.

4-40. Outer evaluation as fact and inner evaluation as truth

As a terrestrial life entity, our consciousness has been subordinated to the physical domination structure by genetic domination in each era, shouldering the two major desires, the domination desire and the material desire, as a fate, and directed to the principle of evil competition according to the acquisition competition for others' evaluation for the excessive physical world benefits. For example, since many people believe that a higher rated school has higher evaluation from others, lots of mothers in the lower spiritual dimension who have strong possessive thoughts toward their children are going to treat the children like their personal belongings for Self-desire and Self-satisfaction.

Those who are in the higher rated school might be intellectually superior, but it has no relationship to their real personality formation at all. They may even go to a famous elementary school, junior high school, high school, university and graduate school, with high ranking, but driving to the academic supremacy principle centered only on physical world benefits only instills wrong values. They make the purpose and value of life directing to the physical world benefits, aim for a workplace and a profession of social authority and vested interests, so they raise their children to develop fierce acquisition competition for status, in order to become a winner on the battlefield in the selfish society. If children do not become as their parents wish, the core of ONSHU bursts open, the parent-child relationship is in a specific kind of fierce anger, and it will become the worst parent-child relationship, such as withdrawal or domestic violence.

People aim for a high position because they believe a manager has a higher evaluation than others and a higher salary than low rank employees, so you aim to be a manager rather than a section chief, a section chief instead of a general manager, an executive director more than an executive vice president, and so on. They are acquiring the evaluation from others to gain dominating power. They make desperate efforts to increase things, as they are occupied or cursed by something, being a slave for the instinctive survival consciousnesses, which they will lose eventually and even become obstacles and troublesome in the spiritual world.

Since the dominating desire is supported by the power which is preserved in vested interests, and based on the motivation of wishing to belong on the dominator side, the social system has continued to follow the pyramidal dominating structure in history by the dominator side at the top, in which the dominated side at the skirts is subordinate. However, even though the person obtained the status as CEO, he/she will be an ordinary person after resignation. Even if they gain mountains of materials, they can only use a

Chapter Four ☆ The Conclusion

limited amount for food, clothing and shelter. They cannot wear 100 different clothes at one time, cannot eat 100 meals at one time or live in 100 houses at one time. No matter how much they obtain status, honor and materials, they will lose everything, including their body, when they die. So, it is important for us to be well aware of how the social system in this life functions.

Many people are falling into a "good child syndrome" by worrying about people's evaluation of them. So they end their life with absence of themselves. Their life is not for themselves, but for their superiors, their company, their promotion, deceiving themselves for Self-defense, and saying it is for the sake of somebody or something, and dying not being true to themselves. However, even though they live for the company or their superiors, when they are rejected by the company or the superiors the delusions of the imaginary world of false life become the ONSHU, so that they are tormented by Self-hatred, Self-denial and Self-escape, and at last, will invite Self-destruction such as suicide, which is the worst result of Self-injurious behavior.

For whom are they living their life? Is it for them or is it for somebody else? It will be the important concept for the way of life not to be superintended by the value of the social environment, but to establish the real view of life and death by drawing the separation borderline between oneself and others for the existing purpose and the existing value of life. If the company or your superiors give you a life and make you alive, then the company or your superiors should be the absolute presence for you.

However, you are given a life and are alive now by SHINSEI. *Evaluation from others is only a fact of irresponsible and objective evaluation. On the other hand, since Self-evaluation is always accompanied with Self-responsibility, it is truth based on subjective evaluation.*

Suppose you are affected by a serious incurable disease and you are told by a doctor that your life expectancy is only one month. At that time, if you are at the mercy of that fact, which is *the presence of the phenomenon based on things,* and bear a grudge against the illness and become pessimistic about it, holding anxiety and fear toward the death of the body, and spend your time with unpleasant feelings, it is up to your Self-determination by Self-responsibility, based on your free intention. However, it is also up to your Self-determination by Self-responsibility that you spend every day with gratitude and happiness, by sympathizing with life and death at the same time, based on the rule of "the attainment of the spiritual being during life" by truth, which is *the presence of the consciousness based on SHINSEI.*

Nobody can violate your consciousness and the right to determine based on free intention because it is given by the principle of nonaggression and nonintervention based on the rule of the universe. Therefore, no matter what kind of diagnosis a doctor makes, it is only guided to irresponsible objective evaluation. The doctor does not give you your life, you are not alive by the doctor, and the doctor does not guarantee the spiritual life. Therefore, nobody can stand or intervene between you and *your determination of intention, because the principle of equation based on the rule of freedom exists in the cosmological evidence, by the principle of nonaggression and nonintervention.*

The important point here is, *being dominated by the objective*

Chapter Four ☆ The Conclusion

evaluation from others means to conflict with the fundamental rule of freedom in the universe, so you abandon freedom and lose it by yourself. No matter how others make the objective evaluation, it is totally up to their freedom and their own convenience.

However, Self-evaluation is the subjective evaluation, so you shoulder a fate to bear Self-responsibility. Because of the fate of the earth star, it is unfortunate, but the physical senses continue to direct the arrows to the outside and we are tamed by physical domination, so we *tend to put the value outside ourselves, violate the separation borderline between ourselves and others, being caught by unimportant matters, and live a life to lose essential values.* As a result, we are dominated by the excessive physical world benefits, are superintended by the objective vague evaluations, make effort to increase something we lose, live a life for the physical world benefits by this life and of this life, and at last end with emptiness, no sense of accomplishment, a meaningless and valueless life.

It is important to direct the purpose of life, which is to live for eternal value, to Self-Enlightenment and spiritual evolution, which are the internal world of the separation borderline. We should not be caught by the physical world benefits more than necessary, and find the real view of death and life beyond the verge of life and death, so that it is not to be dominated in consciousness for the excessive physical world benefits and the irresponsible objective evaluation from others, and not become engaged in the acquisition competition for others` evaluation. If you live that way, your life becomes uncertain and you will fall into mental and physical illness, commit Self-injurious behavior by Self-hatred and Self-denial, and direct yourself to Self-destruction.

The arrows of life should be directed to ourselves, and make Self-effort to raise Self-evaluation, establish Self-subjective evaluation based on the meaningful and fundamental value, and make the individual Self-creation based on Self-acceptance, and by Self-affection and Self-affirmation which is the Trinity of love, gratitude, and happiness, and achieve Self-evolution and make the Self-effort for Self-completion.

In the PARAREVO theory, there are always Logos called *"SELF"* existing. The way of life with the subject of "I" is the innermost secret for the way of life of PARAREVO, and also the innermost secret to live an elegant and wonderful life, and the most comfortable and simplest way of life.

4-41. The foundation of the Constitution is established by religions

In the world there are various cultural spheres such as Jewish, Islamic, Christian, Buddhism, Hindu and Confucian. It was the religions that accomplished the central role to establish the cultural environments. In history, the religious theoretical frameworks and values performed mental education, formed the societies, the ethnic groups, the nations, and the cultural spheres in each country.

It is also fact that conflicts and wars have been repeated on countless occasions because of the differences in the cultural theoretical frameworks and values, in history. For the nation, life, estate, and security are guaranteed under the constitution, and the nation is composed with harmony and order. For the social order in the national society, the laws are enacted under the constitution, not

Chapter Four ☆ The Conclusion

by religions. Rules and regulations are enacted under the laws, and treaties are enacted in the international society. The nation makes the national criteria and the national administration based on the constitution, and all systems in the nation are operated under the constitution. People share all life patterns, from school education, social life and order, and food, clothing, and shelter, also culture and civilization, under the constitution, so, it can be said that the constitution itself plays a central role for the national sovereignty.

The draft of the constitution was established with the culture which centered the religious background as a standard. The central standard for the constitution in the world is drafted and enacted by the religious theoretical framework and value of each nation. The constitution in the Christian cultural sphere is enacted with Christianity as the center, Islamic nations enact it with Islam, Hindu nations enact it with Hinduism, Confucian nations enact it with Confucianism, and in Japan, the Meiji Constitution also drafted the Emperor system by the theoretical framework and value by Shinto during the Meiji Restoration, and was enacted by the Meiji government.

The Japanese Constitution that was prepared after World War II was drafted and enacted in three days, and was based on the Pennsylvania state laws at that time, which were executed as liberal laws and rooted the most Christian spirit in the United States, under the direction of MacArthur and GHQ. By this intention, they tried to change the Meiji constitution itself before an autonomous constitution was enacted, by dissolving the mental culture under the name of the constitution, and tried to educate Japanese people by the mental culture of Christianity. The subject which made the backbone of the Japanese spiritual traditions meaningless was the Pennsylvania state laws at that time, which had strong liberal colors based on American Christianity, chanting loudly only for freedom and equality without responsibility, and only insisting irresponsible freedom.

Japan still applauds it ignorantly as the peaceful constitution of the nation. However, this constitution was made to destroy the wonderful mind of loyalty of the Japanese nation and mental tradition which was established to respect the purposes and values of the whole instead of the individual. As a result, school education was getting worse and the sense of morality in youth fell to disorder. It seemed that sexual disgrace could not be stopped. The sexual culture went to low corruption, and the national sense of morals and ethical standard became poor. Only the competition principle of evil was enhanced, and continued to give impetus to the moral hazard for the entire society. So, I could say that Japan is the most Christianized nation in the world without Christian belief. Japanese are dominated by an irresponsible liberal constitution with Christianized humanitarianism, and operating with wrong freedom and equality.

Freedom without responsibility is equal to violence, and many youths who abandoned the principle of Self-responsibility are everywhere, and the social differentials and poverty are increased by disorderly inequality, and invite corruption and confusion of politics and economy. Even though we try to solve various problems of children, family and society, by religions and the spiritual world, the effects are small compared to the constitution, it is like "pouring water on a hot stone." Even if you participate in a new religion and do your best to conduct religious faith, it only makes more problems and you will not reach any solution but only build the chain of unhappiness.

In order to regenerate the good spiritual tradition of the Japanese nation, which has been built by the spiritually wise Japanese women, we should dispose of this constitution which was pressed down by the theoretical framework of monotheism, and enact an autonomous constitution, as soon as possible.

4-42. The 20th century was the era of ideological strife

In the 20th century, under the structure of conflict between capitalism and communism, revolutions and wars have broken out all over the world. The birth of the communist ideology gave its first cry from a rehashing of religious theory of Judaism and Christianity.

Karl Marx sincerely respected his father who was a devout Jewish believer. However, when the wind of the persecution of Jews in Europe blew, his father gave up Judaism very easily and converted to Christianity. For such an act of betrayal by his father, Marx turned from feelings of reverence to the opposite ONSHU, became skeptical, and started to think that even God was only a delusion produced by human wisdom. He completely denied theism, which was the world of mind and soul, and tried to define the value only in materialism, which was the visible material world. As a result of the creation, the theoretical framework and value of dialectical materialism was made.

So, I could say that the root of Marx`s ideology was a rehashing theory of vengeful thoughts and challenges against Judaism and Christianity, which was born from *the core of ONSHU of the parent-child relationship.* There are many facts that children terminated their parents in the communist revolution. So it proves that the facts started from this motivation and cause, according to the PARAREVO theory.

The communist ideology was a contradictory theory with capitalism created from the ONSHU and vengeful thoughts toward Judaism and Christianity. However, struggles due to the differences of ideology were globally calmed by the collapse of the Soviet Union. Some nations in Asia still advocate the communist ideology. However, at this point, since communism in the Soviet Union collapsed, the capitalism of the United States also collapsed synchronically and simultaneously based on the rule of entropy relativity. In fact, the American economy now days has lost its` substance and seems to be struggling for the final survival.

4-43. The 21st century is the era of religious strife

The first year of the 21st century, on September 11, 2001, a new struggle era began with the terrorist attacks in New York and Washington DC, as the ignition point. We have entered into a new struggle era due to the differences in the religious theoretical frameworks and values in Christianity and Islam.

When we were in the Cold War era between the Soviet Union and the US, it was the conflict axis of ideologies between the nations, so we were able to conclude by the state unit whether it was an allied country or a hostile country, and we could keep the balance by the

Chapter Four ☆ The Conclusion

threat of the nuclear retaliation of one against the other. However, a new elusive and invisible struggle with enemies called terrorists, with their suicide bombing techniques, is extremely difficult to defend against. Their destructive activities are developed very easily enabling them to spread their invisible threat all over the world.

Human beings had already committed big mistakes twice. The first one was on August 6, 1945 in Hiroshima and the second was on August 9, 1945 in Nagasaki. There is an old saying that things always happen in threes. After opening "Pandora's box" called a nuclear bomb, numbers of nuclear bombs have been produced and those could annihilate hundreds of thousands of stars like the earth. Nuclear fingerprints have revealed the fact that nuclear bombs have spread throughout the world by black marketers, after India and Pakistan acquired it in 1995. Iraq changed their policy in 1991 to buy ready-made nuclear weapons at a low price, rather than shouldering economic burden and risks to develop nuclear weapons under the supervision of IAEA and the Unites States. It was because, after the collapse of the Soviet Union, there were many small countries which were separated and became independent, and nuclear weapons were ignored and left in those poor countries, and were sold on the black market and at a low price. Those ready-made nuclear weapons were easy to hide anywhere.

It is certain that the proliferation of nuclear weapons has extended to terrorists, and it is reality on the earth star that we are shouldering this risk which exists at this moment. You might think that we are not so foolish, however, history has proved that human beings are foolish animal.

Since human beings reign on the top of the food chain, it proves that we are the most greedy, sinful and dangerous creatures on the earth. Even now, wars, which are like the Crusades era, actually keep happening, and fanatical fundamentalists who have fallen under the spell of extremely dogmatic religion, proceed behind the scenes with invisible threats. With the theoretical framework and value of existing religious doctrines, it is clear that we are not able to find the clues to solve this problem.

4-44. The 21st century is the era to release from religious spell

As a perspective of the 21st century, human beings should reconsider the religious theoretical frameworks drastically and shift to the cosmological theoretical frameworks and values, to the paradigm revolution. In order to change the existing religious theoretical frameworks and values fundamentally, avoid the crisis of downfall by religious struggles, and build the real collaboration world, we have no choice but to see the reality of the earth from the universal dimension and convert to the theoretical frameworks and values based on the cosmological evidence.

Religions are causing problems of serious religious terrorism and have become the greatest threat socially, ethnically, nationally and even globally. This problem will never be solved unless we clarify who is the subject in your life, religion or "I." If religion is the subject of life, life itself is directed to the religious leader's suggestion and it will become the absolute goodness, even though it is a terrorist or antisocial criminal action.

Chapter Four ☆ The Conclusion

Religions direct you to anxiety and fear by Self-righteous theoretical framework and value, Self-trapping and brainwashing you to personality disorder, making it impossible for you to live without depending on a crutch called a religious order. Religious groups use a carrot called salvation and a stick called fear skillfully, directing to religious dependence, and brainwashing to the parasite syndrome (dependence syndrome). The reason they take away the role and the responsibility of each person to be independent and direct them to not be able to obtain freedom, is because religions play the role and the responsibility as a guard in the prison star. By being at the mercy of past facts such as Allah, Shiva, Jesus, Buddha, or the Bible, Buddhist scriptures and sutra, which are various external gods and saviors created by human beings, we are not living in truth at the present, according to the principle of dimensional domination by external separation, which invites victim consciousness and religious dependence by shifting responsibility.

Spiritual evolution is carried through the rule of reincarnation by the rule of causality of the spiritual consciousness entity, based on the rule of "spirit is subjective and body is objective," and the physical evolution is carried through the rule of genetic chain by the rule of physical causality, based on the rule of "body is subjective and spirit is objective." Since we do not understand the fundamental difference of those rules, we do not have the Self-awareness which our own soul was born with, or Self-determination to select our own DNA and parents, we are not able to achieve the principle for Self-responsibility toward the cause and the subjectivity of life. So, we are not able to live in truth at the present because we are being mind-controlled by the untruth and fabrication of the religious theory, and are being made fools of by the facts in the past.

All facts in the phenomena which might happen in life are manifested by truth, which is the presence of the consciousness based on SHINSEI. The purpose for life is a preparation period for the spiritual life, and in order to obtain true freedom we should be released from physical domination based on the true view of life and death. And Self-completion of the responsibility for each person to be independent by truth and not to depend on anything is the best method to draw the separation borderline between oneself and religions.

4-45. Religion exists in our individual truth

Since the rule of causality of religious theory based on the earth logical evidence is proven as the rule of the genetic chain based on the rule of "body is subjective and spirit is objective," by genetic engineering, it exposes religious doctrines as being untrue, fictitious, and fraudulent theories.

In the PARAREVO theory based on the cosmological evidence, all things are Self-completed and directed to the spiritual dimension of the spiritual world based on Self-responsibility by Self-determination with free intention, according to the rule of reincarnation based on the rule of "spirit is subjective and body is objective." For all results of the cause, problem, and assignment existing in the truth of oneself, the rule of freedom is guaranteed by securing Self-responsibility, according to *the principle of nonaggression and nonintervention* in which even God does not intervene.

If there is a religion which is the origin of teaching, it is not the

Chapter Four ☆ The Conclusion

external god like the religious groups have created, but exists in truth of each person. If you believe there is an external god, it is only your belief or speculation by a brainwashing trick, equal to a fantasy play world. *If you are not able to release religious curse, it shows that your personality and spirituality are in an extremely lower spiritual dimension based on the poor and ugly personality formation history.* Those who are in a higher spiritual dimension are released from religious curse immediately. On the other hand, those who are in a low spiritual dimension carry out religious dependence stubbornly. You are able to obtain real freedom when you accomplish Self-responsibility to become independent, based on truth, which is to not be dependent on anything and not be dominated by anything, and have courage to draw the separation borderline between yourself and religion.

Since the universe is led by Self-management by Self-determination and Self-completion by Self-responsibility, based on the rule of freedom, and based on the principle of equality, all things are equal.

4-46. Religious dependence and shifting responsibility by victim consciousness

People who live the way of life of PARAREVO *carry out the undeniable existentialism, accept the existential presence and phenomenon as they are, unconditionally and totally, and love them from the bottom of their heart as they are by Self-effort.* Those who depend on religions *are not able to live with the clear existentialism, so they Self-escape in to the world of delusions, such as religious groups*. The main reason they have dependence on religions is the result of the theory of Self-hatred and Self-escape. Since they are not able to follow the equation of the spiritual evolution, which releases ONSHU by loving the ONSHU, such as between parents and children, brothers and sisters, husband and wife, and mother or father-in-law, where the core of ONSHU exists, they are not able to love the ONSHU, but instead, seek for a shelter to escape from the ONSHU which is the assignment of life, and find the religious groups which welcome them kindly with untruth and fabrication.

Religious doctrines are good at defining all things for their convenience, so when good things happen, they show off the legitimacy and authority of the doctrines of the religious order, patronize the benefits, and direct to salvation by other hand, but when bad things happen, they drive the person into a corner of liability saying that it is because of the lack of your faith, your poor past life, your lack of propaganda, or not enough offering and donation, etc. It is the art of coaxing of the religious groups to make an excuse for everything for their convenience. So it is the world of religions which are the unsubstantial virtual world, that define both good phenomena and bad phenomena for their convenience. Since religions can easily direct to the virtual world, it is easy to control people's mind.

They are good at using their religious orders to invoke the wrongdoer consciousness and the victim consciousness, and shift responsibility to others and it will be released from both your liability and the principle of Self-responsibility. They take advantage of your Self-centered mind, Self-defense, and Self-escape, and implant anxiety and fear by Self-righteous and peculiar doctrines of the

Chapter Four ☆ The Conclusion

religious orders. They gradually tie you up with a rope of anxiety and fear, getting you busily engaged in offering and donation, not thinking about your family, but instead, devoting in yourself to the religion.

The more you become involved in religious activities, the more you build the chain of unhappiness by negative spiral in the family. You make an arbitrary assumption that even though you fulfill your faith, still unhappy things continuously happen, so if you leave the order, what kinds of unhappiness will occur? You exacerbate further anxiety and fear all the more, and become enslaved by the order, so you are not able to listen to other opinions, are not able to see reality, and think only in the narrow view of the order.

Up to the 20th century, the reason many counterfeit religious groups have grown is because of many false followers who were Self-centered and dominated by physical world benefits, and occupied with Self-defense, according to the mental habit by intentionality of human beings based on the instinctive survival consciousnesses. According to the relative wave based on the spiritual dimension and the rule of groups by the relative original power, *people in the low spiritual dimension gather in the religious order in the low spiritual dimension*. When we catch a glimpse of the nature of the spiritual dimension of the followers, we can see the spiritual nature and the characteristics of the religious group.

Another mental habit by intentionality of human beings is, like the old saying "the misery of others is as sweet as honey," the bad rumor is easy to spread, so the same thing could happen with the many religious doctrines and the orders that the lower in the spiritual dimension they are, the wider and bigger they spread and become. In the news media, and general conversation and gossip in public, they talk about accidents, incidents, disasters and crimes, or gossip about celebrities and others. The gossip about misfortunes of people and disasters quickly become a hot topic and spread in the public in an instant.

The good topics are hard to spread. Why is that? It is because "the happiness of others becomes a source of jealously." When a thing is more genuine and there is more truth in it, it will become more difficult to spread. Up to the 20th century was the era that fake flourished. However, in the 21st century, each person makes Self-effort for their own Self-Enlightenment and spiritual evolution, directing themselves to a higher spiritual dimension without depending on religions and others, in order to complete the existing purpose and the existing value of life, by the PAREVO theory.

4-47. Religious dependence and chain of unhappiness

The structure of the way people fall into religious dependence and religious order are very similar to the situation where people who develop mental illness depend on the hospital and medicines. For example, when the people who suffer from mental disorders such as schizophrenia, severe depression, and anxiety neurosis are told by the doctor that this disease cannot be cured and they must deal with it and take the medicines for the rest of their life.

At first, they would feel a shock because they could not be cured forever, then they are prescribed the medicines, the three "sacred treasures," tranquilizers, antidepressants, and sleep-inducing drugs. Those are the customary antipsychotics. At first those seem

Chapter Four ☆ The Conclusion

to work because of the "Surprising Phenomenon," however, when they continue to take the drugs, their body will become used to the medicines. Gradually, the effects of the medicines weaken, and the doctor prescribes new and stronger drugs, and the amount of medicines increase more and more. The medicine carries the risk of side effects, and the patients are the ones who receive and shoulder the risk, and the doctor does not take any responsibility at all. When we cross the border between the medicine and the risk, we will develop another disease, such as liver dysfunction or autonomic neuropathy from side effects. We will lose the distinction of whether we suffer from the disease or from the risk of the medicine.

When we interchange this phenomenon with religious groups, it becomes similar and easier to understand. The consciousness of the anxiety and fear become the cause of the motivation, and you are directed to the principle of dependence and the domination, and bring about the result of inviting the chain of unhappiness by yourself. This is because *the consciousness and the motivation will follow you until the end.* Therefore, you should not transfer the right of determination and the right of management of your life to religious groups and doctors.

Sometimes, religious dependence might lead to criminal activities such as doing drugs, because the stricter the commandments are by absurd, untruth, and fabricated doctrines, and the more restricted the freedom is, the stronger the curse of the religion becomes and the dependence of the followers toward the order and the domination becomes stronger in the bidirectional way. If the cult religion with reigns of the guru who is a pseudopodia fantastical type or a megalomaniac type person, such as saying that he is the reincarnation of Buddha, the second coming of Jesus, the final liberation, etc., it often engages in political intervention actively, expands election campaign actively, and leads to confusion of the principal of separation of government and religion. Originally, the purpose of religion and the purpose of politics were completely opposite and were inconsistent in the direction of the value, however, the more dictatorial the guru of the religious group is and the stronger his domination desire, the more the group has a tendency to become involved in politics.

So, if you have courage and draw the separation borderline between yourself and the religious group clearly, you will surly recover the harmony and order of yourself and your family and you will *have a life and creation of family of happiness based on free love.*

4-48. The vertical and horizontal personality formation history

As I mentioned earlier, the prenatal environment and the family environment establish the base of the personality formation history, and the greatest influence in the personality formation history is the sentimental relationship of vertical love and ONSHU with the parents. It is because this relationship connects through to the sentimental affinity up to love of SHINSEI, which is the fundamental creation original power in the universe, according to the basic principle to make the core of vertical love and ONSHU.

According to the rule of balance and the rule of negative and positive, boys try to form the personality balance of a higher spiritual dimension by maternal love, and girls try to form the personality balance of a higher spiritual dimension by paternal love. Then, based on the basic principle of horizontal love in the marriage couple, it connects to the sentimental affinity of love of opposite negative and positive in the universe.

In order to achieve Self-completion of love and ideal personality formation in vertical and horizontal, everybody has been seeking the ideal parents, married couple and family; however, as yet nobody has ever really confirmed the existence. If a person like a saint had manifested the form of love and ideal couple as a role model substantially in the world, this world would not be like it is today. Even if he has been called a saint, there is no way for a single man as the relative objectivity, to accomplish the ideal love world by himself.

4-49. Prenatal environment and the ground environment of saints are paradox

We all descended to this world again seeking a good family environment and good life experiences. Nobody seeks poor environment and experiences. The saints and righteous persons in history not always had a comfortable and peaceful life. Many saints and righteous persons surpassed the poor parent-child relationship, the family environment and life experiences by love and overcame their trials and tribulations, and might have spiritually awakened after going through all sorts of hardships. Jesus grew up as an illegitimate child with a step-father, Gautama Siddhartha (Buddha) grew up with a step-mother, and some of the historical saints and righteous persons were illegitimate or adopted children or some of them were confined during childhood. It is not too much to say that none were brought up with love from decent parents.

When I see the personality formation history of the greatest saints and righteous persons, they had unusual backgrounds, and the common factor was the existence of the greatest mothers. The framework of the spiritual consciousness entity, which became the core of their personality, was made for the spiritual quality improvement and the physical condition improvement by maternal love, based on the rule of change by birth and re-birth in the prenatal life, and then they were born to this world.

Therefore, the level of the spiritual dimension based on the mental world and the personality dimension of the mother before her pregnancy and during pregnancy have a great influence. I can imagine that the spiritual dimension of Mary, the mother of Jesus, and Maya, the mother of Gautama Siddhartha, was extremely high in that era. Jesus and Gautama descended to this world and spent the ideal and loving prenatal life, and were born to this world by the real equation of spiritual evolution, based on the rule of change by birth and re-birth. However, in the ground life, they were born as illegitimate children and had grown up in a poor life and family far from the love and ideal family.

The equation of spiritual evolution will be completed by two conditions: first, the principle of Self-responsibility *to release ONSHU (the "body mind") by loving the ONSHU,* and the second, we must realize that *ONSHU is the closest presence by the rule of exclusion theory by jealousy.* This is because the two totally opposite equations for spiritual evolution, the prenatal life of love and the

Chapter Four ☆ The Conclusion

ground life of trials and tribulations based on the rule of entropy relativity, are directed by the rule of change by birth and re-birth.

4-50. Habit of mind is inherited from mother

Since most mothers in this world are ignorant and do not understand that their womb is the sanctuary for the rule of change by birth and re-birth, many of them conduct lustful sexual relationships which is on the extension thought of sexual disgrace by undifferentiated sexual desire consciousness, rather than a sacred conception relationship. When most women are pregnant, they bear children instinctively according to the social custom.

Those mothers entrust the most important conception relationship and the pregnancy period, which is the equation for spiritual evolution based on the rule of change by birth and re-birth, to medical common sense theory and without any Self-effort to achieve the role and responsibility as a mother, toward her fetus. The fetus inherits the poor mental habit of those mothers, and is born to this world as *a product of the foolish mother.*

Many parents might think that children can be raised after birth, however, the mother's mental habit is already inherited before the birth. We often hear that "the children do not listen to what the parents say but do what the parents do." Because of this, most parents and children are not able to draw the separation borderline between the parents and the children and lose the integrity by interfering with the rule of freedom. They become dependent on each other, lose the spiritual intelligence, fall into parasite syndrome (being unable to be independent), and lose social intelligence and healthiness. As a result, many children become withdrawn, or fall into NEET (not in employment, education or training) and narrow their place in society by themselves and lose it eventually. In the course of time, they may cause personality damage, and their feelings toward the parent-child changes to hatred, and they abuse each other, criticize each other, and those actions often transform to domestic violence, negative mental disorders of schizophrenic type, anorexia and social phobia caused by bullying.

This is caused by the ignorance of the parents, and the number of children who spend their life like a *living corpse* is increasing rapidly. So I must say that *ignorance is the shadow of death, and does not produce any emotion, and being alive is just a term but they are actually dead.*

In order to not be like this, we should draw the separation borderline between ourselves and others even though we are the parent and child, give up each possession concept and dependence, and clarify the cause and the subjectivity in the rule of causality based on the PARAREVO theory. We should become aware of the thought that *children were born to this world by selecting their parents and devoting themselves to their parents, and complete the spiritual evolution.* They will never be disobedient to their parents causing spiritual degeneration.

Even though parents are always directing the consciousness to their children, they should avoid interfering more than necessary, and not raise them with just words, kindness and economic power, but to complete the role and the responsibility to raise their children by showing themselves as a role models with ideal love of SHINSEI unity.

Chapter Four ☆ The Conclusion

Parents must raise their children to live by the principle of Self-responsibility, from their early childhood. In order to do so, they have to clarify the cause, the problem, the assignment, and the subjectivity toward the life, and teach them "you were born to select mother and father as your parents, and you also decided your life by yourself. Your life is totally up to your free intention, and you should make the Self-effort to shoulder the responsibility and become independent."

The parents should leave all decisions for the life of their children to their children's free intention, and the parents should also make the Self-effort to let their children shoulder rigorous Self-responsibility according to *the principle of independence of love and freedom, not to the principle of dependence on kindness and domination. It means that the parents raise their children to carry out the attitude to accept as they are, unconditionally and totally, with gratitude and happiness, all phenomena and matters regarding their life. As a result, the parents will be released from all responsibilities and distresses toward their children, and the children will be released from all dependences and ONSHU toward the parents.* The parents and children have to reaffirm this all the time with each other, and make Self-effort to deepen the independence, understanding and consensus of each other, in order to not fall into shifting responsibility by victim consciousness and dependence syndrome. By each of them achieving Self-independence, they will make Self-completion of the real Self-responsibility, and it will lead to obtaining real freedom.

To intervene with children, there are "a hundred negatives and not a single positive," so even though they are the parents-child, they should draw the separation borderline between oneself and others and define the cause and the subjectivity by the rule of spiritual causality based on the PARAREVO theory, and complete their role and the responsibility for each other.

4-51. Roles and responsibilities of a couple with ideal love

In the parent-child relationship, children shoulder Self-responsibility for the assignment and duty toward the spiritual evolution of their life. The role and responsibility for parents is to prepare the body and receive the soul of the child, as the result of their sexual relationship. They have the duty and the responsibility to offer the maternal love in the prenatal life and, raise healthy children who will be able to adapt to various societies and environments.

Another important responsibility for the parents is surpassing the hard feelings toward each other and sharing the common purpose of their life and value, and achieving the personality formation as a married couple that establishes the sentimental sphere of ideal love of SHINSEI unity. The role and responsibility for a married couple is to direct the existing purpose and value of each other to Self-Enlightenment and spiritual evolution, to a higher spiritual dimension. They should not turn their attention only to the children, but create true ideal love of the couple by their Self-effort.

They should direct their consciousness to try to establish the personality balance of negative and positive, in feminine negative nature and masculine positive nature, all the time, and build Self-integration based on the PARAREVO theory.

4-52. Material wealth produces poor mind

We human beings have a depth consciousness memory, in which we decided our parents and descended to this world, so, if we can confirm it and be assured of that memory somewhere in our life, we will have a completely different view of life.

The poor family environment and the relationship between the parent-child would not necessarily function as minus factors, but would make stronger the bonds of love and let you realize the preciousness and tenderness to live. In the economically rich environment, the material intervention becomes stronger between the parents and child, and the soul and the body, so it would be harder to attain spiritual enlightenment because of the material satisfaction in this life, and the way of spiritual evolution would be closed, which would be rather unfortunate for the person.

More children in the developing countries, like Japan used to be, are more devoted to their parents with higher mentality and reliability than those in the advanced nations. Even though the parents can't give plenty of the materials to their children, the bonds of love between the parents and the child are stronger.

According to the rule of "spirit is subjective and body is objective," the advanced nations are being forced to decrease the birthrate. This is brought about by the poorness of mind due to material wealth. In the economically poor developing countries, the parents can only give to their children a little breast milk and love. I have heard disgusting stories that in some advanced nations selfish mothers are using a nursing bottle to pour the breast milk and give it to their children, without maternal love, because the shape of their breast would become bad due to breast-feeding. I am even more astonished to hear that some doctors guide such things openly. Because they raise the children not by love but by money, the declining birthrate certainly occurs. Under an economically wealthy environment, parents have more time and money, so they easily interfere and intervene in their children's lives more than necessary and force their purpose and value on the children. As a result, they take away the opportunity for the children to be independent and acquire freedom, and increase the dependence syndrome.

The only purpose for the rule of reincarnation is to complete Self-Enlightenment and spiritual evolution. The soul, the spiritual consciousness entity, would not choose it's parents in the advanced nations in which they would be satisfied economically but lack love, so there is less opportunity for spiritual evolution. I think this is the main reason for the decline of the birthrate.

In fact, the reason for the decline in the birthrate is not because parents do not want to conceive children; it is because infertile couples, who could not conceive children even if they wish, are increasing. In the developing countries, because of harsh family environments, trials and tribulations are given unconditionally, like many saints had, so people are given more opportunity to be independent by Self-effort, and the possibility for freedom and spiritual evolution.

In the equation for spiritual evolution based on the PARAREVO theory, since the spiritual consciousness entity descend by conception as a predetermination of the rule of reincarnation, for directing to spiritual evolution based on the rule of "spirit is subjective and body is objective," more children are born, despite the environments, to parents in poor and severe situations like the developing countries.

According to the PARAREVO theory, it is not always good to be born in a wealthy family or advanced nation, however, the environment is not really an issue if we practice the way of life of PARAREVO.

4-53. Separation borderline between self and others and true spiritual relationship of parent-child

The rule of the universe and the rule of the earth are defined based on the opposite and paradoxical rule, and even in the intangible substantial world and the tangible substantial world, the vector is directed in totally opposite directions.

It is fact that the mother and father are physical parents; however, the truth is that the soul's parents are SHINSEI. According to the principle of dimensional integration, the body is alive by the relative original power with the soul, and the soul is alive by the relative original power with SHINSEI.

We should aim for personality formation of SHINSEI unity, in which SHINSEI, the spiritual consciousness entity, and the body, are integrated in the Trinity. So, we should establish the integrity to direct to the relative subjectivty based on the principle of dimensional integration, in which the body is integrated to the spiritual consciousness entity, the spiritual consciousness entity is integrated to SHINSEI and is directed to the SHINSEI integration consciousness, and practice that way of life.

The fundamental equation for spiritual evolution in which children surpass the parents by love, integrate to fundamental love of SHINSEI of the universe, and achieve the spiritual growth for higher spiritual evolution, the rule of the universe will complete the sentimental relationship between the parents and the children. Therefore, to those who have a grudge against parents, spiritual evolution and the path to live are closed, and they end up inviting Self-destruction.

4-54. Marital relationship is the second ONSHU

The first ONSHU is between the parents and children in the personality formation history, and the next ONSHU is between the marred couple. Nowadays, divorces in the young generation and divorces after a long marriage are becoming a social problem in Japan.

In a consciousness survey of women who are more than 65 years old, regarding their husbands, the result was 85 percent of them felt that the husband was just a housemate and/or were in house separation. Even though they married for love, as time passed they became more hateful of each other and criticized and abused each other. Why do the relationships change? The main reason is their existing purpose and existing value of life for each other is not based on the spiritual benefits beyond the verge of life and death, but they have continued the relationship as a married couple with untruth and fabrication, working together based on the physical world benefits.

Chapter Four ☆ The Conclusion

As a physical nature of the earth star life, the role and the responsibility of each other is clarified by the desire consciousness of the physical world benefits, which are derived from the two major instinctive survival consciousnesses. In Japan, a husband is in complete control of the economy, by the dietary desire consciousness, and a wife raises children and does housework, by the sexual desire consciousness. Also, husband has the right to determine and possess everything, and a wife is forced to be dependent economically and assume a subordinate position. Human history has continued, endlessly, to be directed to this *principle of dependence and domination.* While the wife is dependent on the economy of the husband, and the husband is dependent on the child rearing and the housework by the wife, and by co-depending on each other, they end up taking each other's freedom and restricting each other. As time passes, the wife begins to have a sense of oppression and despair and starts feeling uncomfortable with the existence of the husband.

The ONSHU of love is *deprivation and oppression of freedom.* Therefore, the vertical ONSHU in the parent-child relationship is called the first hatred, and the ONSHU in the relationship of the married couple is called the second ONSHU. In other words, both ONSHU are different. A more concrete explanation is, the parent-child relationship is more like grudge and hatred than ONSHU. It has been brought out from virtual and false conviction caused mainly by the "body mind" based on the earth logical theory. Although we chose our parents by our own decision in the spiritual world, we bear a grudge against them because of our selfish delusion. ONSHU in the relationship of the married couple is the conflict caused by the fluctuation of reality and non-fiction between the "soul mind" and the "body mind" based on the cosmological theory. Married couples should develop love together anew in order to solve the past life relationship.

4-55. Love pair system and the relative original power

In order to release the vertical love, the fundamental love, of ONSHU, we select the parents who are the closest presence in this life, and are born to this world. However, by the ignorant parents' attachment to their children, and their claim for the possession of their freedom, the children are deprived and oppressed. As a result, the children lose the subjectivity and independency, and add more ONSHU toward the parents.

The equation to release ONSHU *("body mind")* is *by loving the ONSHU*. The ONSHU exists near you, and the equation and the answer to release it are always waiting for you in your surroundings. We must understand that ONSHU is given to us as a destiny in order to release ONSHU itself toward all relationships in life.

So, concerning marriage, it is important to make the determination of resolution and Self-effort to complete the principle of Self-responsibility to accept as it is unconditionally and totally with gratitude and happiness, toward the marriage which is by their own determination to be a couple. In order to release the horizontal ONSHU of love of a married couple, the wife and husband make the Self-determination to become a married couple as the closest existence in each other's life. Their souls pledged to meet as fate and live together as the best partners in life before they were born to this world in order to make Self-completion of Self-responsibility to accept all things unconditionally and totally with gratitude and happiness. So they must care and love each other, understand each other and nurture each other in this life, as the ideal married couple of love of SHINSEI unity, no matter what would happen.

The marriage view of PARAREVO is different from the general marriage view of this world. According to the PARAREVO theory, the general marriage in this world is just sharing a house together, and the purpose for the marriage is to have children and raise them as a family, rather than live alone. However, the real purpose for PARAREVO marriage is different. The PARAREVO marriage forms a partnership according to the rule of the universe and based on love with the theory of universe. The couple aim to step up the spiritual dimension together for cosmic life, so it will suggest that their existence is sustainable, forever. This love pair system is the essence of the PARAREVO theory. Since all problems that happen in this world originate in ONSHU between woman and man, I conclude that we are not able to change the world unless establishing the PARAREVO view of a pair system and expand it from the individual level to family, ethnic, national and world level. The problems of love between woman and man make everything in this world very complicated.

A general marred couple, in the beginning, love each other and live together, however, since they do not have true purpose of life together, which is beyond the death and life, many of the couples are realizing the difference in value of each other, increasing distrust, and in many cases, finally divorce by hating each other. It is very ironical that they like each other in the beginning, but they hate each other the most when they split. This type of marriage view is called "marriage view of EROS" by the PARAREVO theory. It is based on the selfish desire of Self-centered egoism which is based on the idea of "I like the person." When they are going to marry they would think that if I marry the person I can be happy. After all, it is the marital image according to the theory created by human beings. This image is only for terrestrial purpose and will collapse as *the theory of desire*. Even if they do not come to hate each other, they would live for a different purpose. For instance, one would be devoted to work and the other would pay attention to the children only, so even they live in the same house their life is based on their own Self desire. Self-desire is not sustainable.

Moreover, in the general marriage in this world, the closer the couple is, when one dies the deeper the sorrow will be for the one left. If we set up the purpose of marriage for life in this world, it will end eventually. Therefore, that love is not sustainable and I have to say that those marriages are just fictional. Anything non-sustainable is not real just like a movie. Love which does not promise eternity is not true love. Thus, when one partner dies, the one left will be sad. Because of the dependence on the partner the one left will fall victim to Self-pity. Since one does not exist for the other, but only for oneself, he/she will be sad when the partner is gone. This is the limitation for a general marriage.

However, this is opposite from the real marriage view of PARAREVO. Since they have a common purpose for marriage life, which is to raise the spiritual dimension together, they won't have different values for the marriage. They understand the relationship of man and woman as positive and negative, and understand that each of them is a valuable existence for the other to become a cosmic

Chapter Four ☆ The Conclusion

entity, so they will never lose interest, start hating each other or have a relationship with someone else. Moreover, when they understand the fundamental existence purpose as a married couple of PARAREVO, they will never be sad when one of them die, because they understand eternal love beyond death. Rather they will be pleased since his/her partner's soul was released from the physical domination of the body. Our soul, the spiritual consciousness entity, will never disappear, so death is not the most unfortunate thing. They will complete their love for the other, thus, they love the other more than they love themselves. The partner does not exist for you, but you exist for the partner. Therefore, they feel pure happiness to the other who set out on a journey to the world of the spiritual consciousness entity by releasing the physical domination.

This feeling is simply based on love for the other, and to make the other happy from the beginning to the end. There is a difference between "I like you" and "I love you." The former is only your unilateral feeling rather than how the other feels. The latter is to think about the other person by being in the other person's position rather than in your own position and care about the other from your heart. This type of marriage is called "marriage view of LOGOS" in the PARAREVO theory. It is based on love with the theory of the universe, which means to comply with the rule and principle of the universe and meet with the reason of the universe. On the other hand, the "marriage view of EROS" is not based on love with the theory of the universe but based on sexual desire, which means not meeting with the reason of the universe.

The PARAREVO theory aims to complete love. The completion of love complies with the rule of negative and positive based on the rule of relativity, and it considers that the love relationship between woman and man is the most fundamental core of love. It also indicates that the individuality is actually formed with two persons, so that a single person, either woman or man, is not considered a completed person, based on the rule and principle of the universe. They are not able to complete love.

Therefore, historical saints and righteous persons such as Jesus and Siddhartha were not able to complete love because they were bachelors. A person who cannot complete love but preaches about love means it is only the theory of Self-satisfaction and narcissism of a single person, and the theory of inconsistence.

However, since Non-PAREVO married couples do not understand the fundamental existing purpose and the existing value of being a married couple, they increase unpleasant feelings toward each other and end up adding more ONSHU. In order for all things in the universe to exist equally, love is constantly poured in the SHINSEI integration consciousness by the influence of the relative universal original power, and all existing things are forced to exist according to each spiritual dimension.

The fundamental rule of the universe is that opposite things, such as plus and minus, negative and positive, stamens and pistils, and female and male, appear synchronically and simultaneously based on the rule of entropy relativity, and direct to the relative subjectivity according to the principle of dimensional integration, and in order to achieve spiritual evolution to a higher spiritual dimension they are systematized as the mechanism of the love pair system, to the entire universe. We human beings are not the exception. According to the rule of relative original power with this love pair system, we are forced to exist and shoulder Self-effort as a fate to form the harmony and order of love integrated into a higher dimension, by both women and men, make the common denominator of SHINSEI, and establish *the love pair system of SHINSEI unity*.

The intention of the universe has led spiritual evolution and physical revolution by directing to women's intention, according to the principle of dimensional integration, by the slight fluctuation of imperfection based on the rule of entropy relativity, with women as the relative subjectivity and men as the relative objectivity. In order to direct evolution to a higher spiritual dimension, women connote the logic of love, integration, harmony, and creation as their nature, and men obtain the logic of power, domination, struggle, and destruction as their nature, and the intention power of women surpasses the intention power of men, and directs to try to complete *regeneration of SHINSEI and soul* to new life entities of the universal dimension by *the rule of change by birth and re-birth*.

The love pair system of SHINSEI unity of women and men is the universal rule of the relative original power, which is fated and unavoidable on this earth star, in order to make the personality formation of love in a higher dimension. By completing this love pair system, it will become possible to form the integrated ideal love sphere structure. So, since the entire universe is integrated by the relative universal original power based on free love, and exists in the SHINSEI integration consciousness world with SHINSEI as the common denominator, all things form the harmony and order by the sphere structure, by each constructing the sustainable sphere structure by the pair system, and are operated by the mechanism which exists eternally.

However, since Non-PARAREVO marriages with no understanding of the existing purpose and the existing value of life is not a true marriage, it is very important for the married couple to understand the PARAREVO theory and go back to the basics and have the courage to start again as an ideal love couple of SHINSEI unity.

4-56. The 4 rules of relativity based on the spiritual dimension

In the pair system, there exists *the rule of relativity* which is the relative wave based on the spiritual dimension, and it divides roughly into four rules.

(1) the rule of relativity of SOSEI (fostering each other)

(2) the rule of relativity of SOKOKU (exhausting each other)

(3) the rule of relativity of SOZO (creation)

(4) the rule of relativity of HAKAI (destruction)

The rule of relativity of SOSEI is a relationship in which the more a couple face each other, the more they are able to take care of each other and make each other's life more alive. This is a relationship in the "Mental lower level dimension," and it makes healthy and wholesome sustainable life, mentally and physically.

The rule of relativity of SOKOKU is a relationship in which the more a couple is involved with each other, the more they quarrel with each other, hate each other and cause trouble for each other, and finally exhaust each other. This is a relationship in the "Astral middle level dimension," and makes an unwholesome and unhealthy life mentally and physically.

Chapter Four ☆ The Conclusion

The rule of relativity of SOZO is a relationship in the "Mental middle level dimension," in which the more a couple is involved with each other the more they treat each other well, love each other, understand each other, and take care of each other, and it is possible to direct to Self-Enlightenment and spiritual evolution by creating a life of love and joy progressively and expansively, and enjoying each individual art.

The rule of relativity of HAKAI is a relationship in the "Astral lower level dimension" where once they are relative, they lose the vitality of life, and no matter what they do they will be directed to destruction. They lose fortune and health, and are driven to Self-destruction such as death by incurable disease, accident or suicide, and have an ugly and poor life with each other.

So, according to the rule of relativity of the pair system, the relative original power based on the spiritual dimension evokes the consciousness, and the words and deeds would be conducted by either motivation of love based on the "soul mind" or ONSHU based on the "body mind." Now, you can understand how the relative original power, by the relative wave of the pair system in the spiritual dimension, has a huge influence on your life. Even though each person has a wonderful and admirable character individually, once they become a husband or a wife, it might be an exhausting relationship with constant discord if their spiritual dimension does not match by the rule of relativity of SOKOKU.

Destiny and fortune are directed and completed according to the relative wave based on the spiritual dimension and the rule of the relative original power of the pair system. However, since the rule of freedom in this world takes priority over the scenario which was anticipated and predicted in the spiritual world, people decides their partner by free intention. Even though the winning ticket is prepared in the scenario, somehow they end up selecting the partner by value of the physical world view and individual preference such as appearance and tastes. Most of them have a tendency to draw a losing ticket, because the value of desire by the excessive physical world benefits and evaluation go beyond the scenario in the spiritual world, and some of them become a husband or a wife merely because of sexual desire, lust, and passion, because of their poor mind.

In the rule of the universe, since the spiritual dimension is the basis for all things, the relative wave is determined based on the spiritual dimension, and the relative original power based on it derives and is directed to all effects. It is because *truth, the presence of the consciousness based on SHINSEI, only exists in the spiritual dimension of each person.* Those who live the way of PARAREVO deal with other people according to the person's spiritual dimension, and do not emit their feelings or empathize more than necessary, and try to accept the presence of the person as he/she is, unconditionally and totally.

4-57. The historical perspective of legalized male dominating structure

The reason women and men have different understandings and position of married life is because an important system is inserted in the mechanism of each role and responsibility for women and men on the earth star. The nature connoted in the consciousness structure of men is derived from the spiritual formation history created by the sexual desire consciousness, which is one of the instinctive survival consciousnesses and has been inherited continuously through the genes from the primitive life entity, and is inserted in the DNA of men. By the selfish theoretical framework and value of the male dominating structure, the history of male heirship has been repeated generation to generation.

For example, the ultimate system of discrimination against women was the struggle for supremacy between the legal wife and the concubines behind the heir problem in Royal family, Shogun family and Imperial family, and it has forced sufferings and conflicts for women, history of enmity in sorrow and ONSHU has built, and such a system still exists today, as an undeniable fact.

And this male type dominating structure has continued for a long time in the married couple, the family, the society, the nation and everything. In the nations and the religious doctrines in which the male type dominating structure, such as polygamy, is legitimated, it is difficult to function by the rule of change by birth and re-birth, so their spiritual evolution would become extremely difficult, and women would be murdered or shut in by the culture and the civilization of the retention of old-fashioned ideas.

The terrestrial life is shouldering the body, as the fate, so we can't survive without food. In order to eat we have to work. In order to work we have to provide time and labor. Therefore, the fundamental cause on the prison planet is that life itself is directed and systematized to inconvenience. The biggest inconveniences in the terrestrial life are labor by the dietary desire consciousness and marriage by the sexual desire consciousness. In this life, we are being systematized by the rule of dimensional domination, in which men dominate the economy to gain daily bread and milk, and women are bound at home on the pretext of child rearing and housework. So, for a long time, the women's path to social independence was closed, and legally, women were dominated by this system. Women were inevitably forced to be in a position in which, without depending on men economically, they could not live, so they were restricted and forced to live an inconvenient life. This historical sorrow and ONSHU of women has been inserted in the genetic consciousness of the brain, according to the rule of physical causality, and inherited throughout history.

Even though the discrimination against women and disparity between men and women in the social advance have mostly gone, lack of love and delicacy toward women, with the words and the deeds of the offensive language of men such as "you must give thanks to me, because I am the one feeding you." This authoritative attitude of men infuriated women and touched off the ONSHU of long standing, and reflects the present times called middle-aged divorce.

In the 21st century, there will be no future for the earth star unless we direct to the drastic theoretical frame work and the value, which convert the discrimination against women and disparity between men and women, into the totally opposite, by the PARAREVO theory.

Chapter Four ☆ The Conclusion

4-58. Love of women and men is the height of "the relative art"

Children chose the parents as the closest existence, in order to release the ONSHU of vertical love, and the married couple selected each other as the second closest existence, in order to release the ONSHU of horizontal love.

A married couple should draw the separation borderline between each other, and in the role to be independent of each other, form the personality improvement of love with Self-responsibility and the personality balance of negative and positive. They should recognize each other as the inevitable partner of the love pair system of SHINSEI unity, and share the existing purpose and the existing value, love each other and understand each other, and then they would manifest the individual art to accept the existence of each other unconditionally and totally with gratitude and happiness. In order to form the personality balance of negative and positive by surpassing and transcending the sorrow and ONSHU of the married couple by love, they should manifest the relative individual art based on free love, which will be sexually integrated in negative and positive at last.

As long as we were born to this earth star, we all must surpass and transcend the ONSHU between women and men, and carry out the personality formation to *complete the sexual integrated life entity of negative and positive* by love of SHINSEI unity, which is by the relative original power derived from the slight fluctuation of imperfection of the antithesis negative and positive, based on *the love pair system of women and men*. Even if they are saints or righteous persons, there is no exception. When men release the sorrow and the ONSHU of women with the deep affection *of Self-sacrifice,* but not by the *hypocrisy of Self-satisfaction,* they can accomplish the role and the responsibility of the earth star.

 The reason men refused women stubbornly, such as not allowing women to enter a sacred area, as if women were dirty by Self-righteous religious theories of men, is because they have to avoid temptation of their undifferentiated sexual desire consciousness, so they must exclude women indiscriminately and escape from their true feelings. In order to privilege the male type dominating structure favorably, men have legalized the exclusive religious doctrines toward women, put a crown called saints on men as they pleased, reined at the top of the religious organizations, built the pyramidal type dominating structure continuously throughout history, and still now men rein at the top in the religious groups. If the unmarried saints were excused as exceptions, it means that the existence of women was denied from the beginning. So, since there was no existence of the saints without the existence of their mothers, the religion and the lineage would have died out and human beings would already be extinct.

 The fingerprint of history has legalized the root of the male type dominating structure in silence by the Self-righteous religious theoretical framework and value of men, in the absence of women who were the relative subjectivity, and formed the core of the culture. Throughout the history of terrestrial life, no one was born from men, but all were born only from women. If the historical saints died and left this world as unmarried single men, without completing the love pair system of SHINSEI unity, by ignoring the existence of women, no matter what they had realized or said, or

Chapter Four ☆ The Conclusion

what kind of great achievements they had accomplished, they must descend to the earth star again and again according to the rule of reincarnation, because they did not release the core of the sorrow and ONSHU of women, which was the most important assignment in the personality formation. So their own role and responsibility to accomplish spiritual evolution by Self-completion of the love pair system of SHINSEI unity and sublimate to a higher spiritual dimension, still remain in this world.

If the people who were called saints recognized a woman they met as their exact "Taiji," which is the core of integration of the negative (women are representative of negative of the universe) and positive (men are representative of positive of the universe) in the universe, as the relative subjectivity and loved the woman as irreplaceable and a representative of one half of the universe ("negative"), integrated that love and completed the love pair system of SHINSEI unity by releasing the principle of dimensional domination on the earth star, and suggested the direction which human beings should have taken, we human beings would have already achieved spiritual evolution to the life entity in a new spiritual dimension, by completing the sexual integration consciousness rapidly with unity of women and men, and by the equation to release the sorrow and ONSHU in love of women and men.

There is a spiritual door to the spiritual world of the universe (the cosmic world) which is emerging from the atmosphere and extends beyond both the intangible and tangible earth. This door does not open unless the key and the keyway of the door exactly match relatively. The key to open *the door to the spiritual world of the universe* is given to men and the keyway is given to women.

Without conquering the steps of spiritual evolution up to the spiritual dimension where the door exists, it is absolutely impossible to open *the door to the spiritual world of the universe.*

Since all souls on the earth star are going to the intangible world of the earth after the body dies, they only return to the tangible world of the earth by reincarnation, so until very recently, no soul has gone to the spiritual world of the universe after graduating from the earth. It is because nobody understands the enigma of the pair system of women and men.

The place where the key and the keyway are given is in the sexual organs. The key is given in the symbol of men, and the keyway is given in the symbol of women. If the key or the keyway are mismatched, or if it is the key of a single man and the keyway of a single woman, "the Heaven (the spiritual world of the universe)'s door" is not going to open. *This key and the keyway are not about merely physical sexual organs, but the secret and the essence to release the undifferentiated sexual desire consciousness are hidden in it, as the untold equation for spiritual evolution.*

People who have sexual relationships with innumerable people and repeat divorce and marriage over and over again the sexual disgrace of undifferentiated sexual impulse with lack of love will be the destruction of the key and the keyway, and will be the greatest Self-injurious behavior toward the spiritual consciousness entity. Since the spiritual key and keyway are the precious treasures to open "the Heaven's door," you should not fall into immoral sexual relationships or sexual delusion.

"The Heaven" is a place for two people, and it is the spiritual world of the ideal spiritual consciousness entity, which was completed in love of women and men of SHINSEI unity and completed the sexual integration based on the love pair system. The love of women and men of SHINSEI unity is the shape and the form of negative and positive which sexually integrated each individual mental entity with true love, with SHINSEI as the common denominator.

The dietary desire consciousness will vanish at the moment we take the body off, however, the sexual desire consciousness is the basic issue of love, and the important mechanism to create universal relative original power of negative and positive of the universe, and the fundamental principle to create the eternal sustainable energy, so it remains as the assignment after taking the body off. It means that unless we surpass and transcend the sexual desire consciousness, which is the instinctive survival consciousness, by love of women and men of SHINSEI unity, "the Heaven's door" will not open.

Jesus and Buddha did not become symbols of religion because they wanted to. They are false images, which were set up by religions by the intention of the male type dominating structure and created for convenience. If not so, the religions could not have built the history as the male centered pyramidal type dominating structure, by ignoring the existence of women.

Because we often misuse the key and the keyway by undifferentiated sexual desire consciousness, it causes disharmony in married couples by building ONSHU as the core of the couple, discord of the family and the discord of the society, and this bad feeling will expand from the nation to the world, making everything complicated, and it becomes the source of various problems. History has shown the fact clearly that the disharmony of women and men became the root of the unpleasant feelings for all things, and the religions could not resolve anything at all even though they have set up the theory of incomplete, unmarried saints and religious founders, who did not even build a heaven in this world, as a role model. When I see the fact that the unmarried society, which was built by the clergy, still reins in the religious world, I strongly feel that the personality deviation is extremely lacking in balance in the religious personality formation history.

The ideal personality formation of love is not formed by religious studies and particular organizations, but all things are formed based on the experiences in a systematic environment, and especially based on women and men and love, harmonious and systematic personality formation of negative and positive is supposed to be done universally. No matter how excellent the person is, like the saints and the righteous persons, they can never complete love alone. To complete love, it is essential to have an ideal partner to derive the universal and sustainable relative original power of the fundamental negative and positive of the universe.

4-59. The time axis is like a virtual world

As I explained previously, our assignment and responsibility is how we have drawn the separation borderline between ourselves and others and established Self-integrity with truth, which was *the existence of the consciousness based on SHINSEI,* toward fact, which was *the existence of the phenomena based on things,* visible incidents, such as the natural environment, social environment, cultural environment, and the mental environment of parent-child and married couple.

Chapter Four ☆ The Conclusion

In the meantime, the time axis is *the virtual world where even fact is not guaranteed* with invisible things like the past and the future, and is the fictitious world led by elusive supposition and speculation. It is very difficult for us to draw the separation borderline between ourselves and the time axis. In fact, we have never drawn it, in the present nor in the past. As a result, we often confuse the true nature by leaving the decision to speculation and supposition.

Because of the consciousness domination of an imaginary phase called the time axis, we are not able to live with truth called the present. *And, the most frightening point of the time axis is it does not even guarantee fact.* There are so many rumors and media reports about unpleasant things because "the misery of others is as sweet as honey." However, we never verify even one matter as fact in that unpleasant information, we just direct ourselves to unpleasant feelings by accepting one-way information unconditionally without any doubt.

When people who live the way of PARAREVO determine or evaluate the right and wrong of things, they guarantee the minimum fact, avoid emitting feelings or empathizing by bringing supposition and speculation in toward the objective fact, such as people's rumors and media reports, and direct it to truth of a higher level by verifying fact only. That is, *they admit the existence of things as the objective fact, but as long as it is not guaranteed in them, they do not accept it as the subjective truth.*

We have been tamed by the virtual world called the time axis, throughout history. All things are directed by the time axis domination, from what time we get up, what time we go to work, what time we go home and what time we go to sleep, to the life styles and the life plans, as is in complete harmony of the past, the present and the future. In the habituation of the time axis domination, we judge the present and even predict the future, based on the facts in the past. We are bringing the past preconception and prejudice to the present, and making the evaluation for persons and society unilaterally. We acquire the habit of mind in which we do not verify and evaluate the present fact correctly and not accept it based on truth. Based on the rule of "body is subjective and spirit is objective," we are tamed by the ghost of the past and the devil of the future called the time axis, which was created by the concept of the memories in the brain before we realized, and unfortunately, our consciousness is completely dominated by delusion and illusion.

Although we seem to live in the present, actually we are living in the world by domination of the past and the future, so unless we draw the separation borderline between ourselves and the time axis of the past and the future, and have the training to live in the present existentially, we fall into domination by the ghosts and devils of the past and the future before we realize and end up living as ghosts in the virtual world without actual conditions.

In fact, this is *the real character of the time axis*. Even though all things change moment by moment, many of us are dominated by the past and the future, so we do not evaluate and accept the present correctly, fall into unpleasant feelings, make our life difficult, and lose our own place. Like this, we are dominated by the consciousness on the extension idea of prejudice and supposition like delusion and illusion of the past, by memories of the brain based on the rule of "body is subjective and spirit is objective" in the continuity of the time axis, so when we evaluate things without guaranteeing the present fact, it points to a totally different truth.

People who live the way of life of PARAREVO make the greatest Self-effort to direct truth to the "soul mind," the relative subjectivity, only for fact, according to the rule of "the attainment of the spiritual being during life" based on the rule of "spirit is subjective and body is objective," in the continuity of zero time period called the present, and direct the intention of determination to a higher spiritual dimension. That is the general concept *of the way of life of PARAREVO, which guarantees the fact of the present and drives to reach truth by carrying through the undeniable existentialism.*

Although we make effort feverishly with unpleasant feelings without gratitude and happiness in the present in order to fulfill the imaginary phase of the future, we only make ourselves fall into Self-destruction but not Self-realization. It is because *the imaginary steps of the future are only the unreal steps no matter how far up you go.* If you want to conquer the top of the mountain and climb by looking only at the top, you will definitely lose your footing and fall down, because you are not seeing the foothold. If you aim for the top, you should step on the ground firmly and climb the present path, step by step.

Going up the substantial steps and completing the Now, is the shortest path for Self-realization, rather than going up the imaginary steps of Self-realization of the future. The existential way is the important technique for life. We should try to preserve the future in the plan but not bring it to the present any more than necessary and live one day at a time achieving Self-completion. This will be important training to acquire such a habit for our life.

We must make Self-completion for things we can do now, and release the acquisition competition for others' evaluation so as not to fall to the good child syndrome by appearances and vanity, and should establish Self-integration. Our responsibility of assignment is to discipline ourselves to draw the borderline with the time axis, firmly, in order to live the precious and irreplaceable life meaningfully and valuably, and achieve Self-completion of *the present* in the substantial world existentially according to the way of life of PARAREVO.

4-60. Evolution is the way to release from the time axis domination

The basis of the mechanism in the history of evolution is nothing but how much we can shorten time and distance and lighten labor. It is because by shortening time and distance, we can release physical labor, and by shortening the distance and the gap of the binding power and the separation space of the body toward the spiritual consciousness entity, the consciousness is restored at zero time period, the Now. This would be the best way to approach the view of the spiritual world in which time does not exist.

Accompanied with the development of science technology, the shortening of time and the release of labor have been done in the history of evolution. As an example, in Japan the transportation method only a few decades ago was by foot or horse. At that time, when people walked from Edo (Tokyo) to Osaka, it normally took more than 20 days requiring lots of labor and time. In the Edo period in Japan, when people wanted to do business in Osaka,

Chapter Four ☆ The Conclusion

they had to consider the situation in Osaka 20 days in the future, however, if we take the bullet train to go to Osaka now days, we can get there in less than 3 hours, so we only need to consider Osaka 2 and half hours in the future.

We have built the rapid civilization, within only a few decades, where automobiles run on the freeway, airplanes fly in the sky, and human beings go to the moon. With the development of nuclear energy we can easily create and provide power. This attempt to reduce physical labor and shorten time by the benefit from the science civilization made great progress in spiritual evolution. *The greatest benefit from the science civilization is the fact that the distance between the spiritual consciousness entity and the body was reduced.* This reduction of time and distance as the method to release the consciousness from physical domination is an epoch-making event.

However, since we have accumulated the process of physical evolution as the genetic information, and inherited it as the memories in the brain, it is not easy to transcend the memories of the time axis. The memories of the brain create the concepts of the time axis, so *when we try directing the function of our brain to the zero time period, the Now, and make Self-effort for existentialism, to manage and complete the consciousness to the undeniable existence, the body is integrated to the spiritual consciousness entity, and it will be easier to aim for spiritual evolution by directing to the rule of "spirit is subjective and body is objective."*

If we can achieve life to complete the consciousness to the Now, the zero time period, by shortening the time axis as much as possible, it comes closer to the rule of "the attainment of the spiritual being during life," and the body exists physically but actually does not exist, so it becomes possible to release from the physical dominating structure which is the instinctive survival consciousness caused by genetic domination, and would be able to prepare to graduate from the earth star. Therefore, when our consciousness makes Self-completion to zero time period, the Now, by drawing the separation borderline toward the past and the future, we will be released completely from the physical body and the material world, and be able to transcend the time axis.

Even though we are in the era of termination with the dropping of the atomic bombs twice in 1945, we have raised the best, incomparable science civilization and developed it. However, by the rule of entropy relativity, the spread of weapons of mass destruction is expanding as an unseen crisis quietly and globally, like a big dark shadow which is totally opposite from bright light.

In order for the world to be united as one, it is not too much to say that now is the time to choose one of the two options. Either the entire nations carry out the consciousness revolution drastically by the new theoretical framework and value, by sharing the common crisis consciousness and transcending all kinds of old theoretical frameworks, such as existing religions, economies, and thoughts, or the crisis of the downfall of the earth becomes absolute under the great sacrifice and we are forced to carry out a reformation.

4-61. Women who are in the high-spiritual dimension are the driving force of evolution

The fate of the earth star has a close relationship with the time axis domination and the physical domination. And by the rule of the relative ground, existing things create their own peculiar power and the direction as the relative original power. Depending on how we connect the relative wave with a higher spiritual dimension, and exercise the consciousness of a higher standard "soul mind" by the relative original power with the relative subjectivity based on SHINSEI, our words and deeds are evoked by the motivation based on free love, and Self-Enlightenment and spiritual evolution are directed to the creation of happiness.

All things in the universe are forced to exist by the relative universal original power as the spiritual comprehensive being, and *it suggests that all existing things have consciousness, thus intention.* All consciousnesses and intentions existing in the universe have a spiritual network with SHINSEI, the verity of the individual entity as a common denominator, and each individual mental entity, the personality and the spirituality, has access or makes a commitment based on the channel of the spiritual dimension.

When the spiritual dimension is different, practical access and commitment becomes one-way only and it would not be interactively. For instance, we human beings cannot make general conversation with minerals, plants or animals. The difference among minerals, plants and animals is determined by rank and position of the spiritual dimension, based on each intention. The rank and position of the spiritual dimension is determined by the speed of the intention and the strength of the intention to be directed to the high spiritual dimension, based on *freedom of the consciousness and the acceptance of love.*

Since the intention of minerals moves in the wave range of

frequency in hundreds and thousands of years, the binding power is strong and we can hardly verify the movement of the mineral itself. Since the intention of plants moves by a much faster frequency compared with minerals, we can observe their growth and various changes in a short period of time, but they still do not reach to the degree of freedom to move by themselves. Animals move with the intention of a much faster frequency compared with that of plants, so they can move freely. In other words, *the degree of freedom of intention and the degree of acceptance of love, suggests and manifests the height of the spiritual dimension.*

This freedom of intention and the acceptance of love have a close relationship with the spiritual dimension, *and the degree of freedom derives from the height and the size of the dimension of consciousness, and the degree of acceptance of love derives from the degree of release of ONSHU connoted in the consciousness.* And those are also determined by whether one is living a Self-centered life for the physical world benefits and merely one's own physical desire, or living for the family, for the ethnic groups, for the nation, for the world, or for the earth. It will make a world of difference, whether one is dominated by physical desire only and lives inconveniently by suppressing the consciousness in a narrow space called an individual, or lives freely by releasing the consciousness to the world and the universe.

When the spiritual dimension becomes higher, reality will become lower. The more we raise the degree of freedom of intention and the acceptance of love, the more the material becomes granulated and waved, and SHINSEI and the spiritual consciousness entity are integrated to the Now, by the pair system, and they will be the eternal existence in the spiritual world of the universe by the sustainable relative original power of SHINSEI unity. In order to do this, we should complete physical evolution by improving our physical condition by genetic recombination in the woman's womb, by the rule of change by birth and re-birth, and according to the principle of dimensional integration by the rule of the relative original power based on the mind and the spirit of the mother, we must complete spiritual evolution by the improvement of spiritual quality.

Therefore, it is no exaggeration to say that evolution is charged with the spiritual dimension of women, because the spiritual dimension based on the mind and the spirit of women directs evolution and degeneration.

4-62. The way of life of PARAREVO transcends the time axis

There are many people in society who say "in reality, nothing can start and nothing can be done without plans and schedules for the near future." It is right, however, it is also an indisputable fact that we are forced to be in agony and have mental conflicts by this time axis, and are directed to not be able to create possibilities of the future.

Why? It is because we are not living the way of life of PARAREVO. Since those who live the way of life of PARAREVO catch *the existence of the phenomenon based on things,* as an undeniable fact, considering this moment as the compilation of the history for evolution, they understand the fact that it is up to each person to achieve Self-management with Self-determination and Self-completion with Self-responsibility based on the rule of freedom, so all things are determined by the present free intention as to how they direct the future by truth which is *the presence of the consciousness based on SHINSEI*.

So, now, regarding an undeniable fact in history, when we direct the consciousness to the "soul mind," as the relative subjectivity based on SHINSEI, according to the principle of dimensional integration, truth can direct the future to evolution and creation. On the other hand, when we direct the consciousness to the "body mind," as the relative objectivity, according to the principle of dimensional domination, truth will direct the future to retrogression and destruction. People who live the way of PARAREVO understand that living individually is the manifestation of the individual art for life. When you can place your life-work in the continuity of something you really like according to the individuality, it will become sustainable and you can have a creative and expansive life without being dominated by the time axis. This is the only method to transcend the time axis.

However, the reality is that you become involved in the work which you do not like and you just continue as a method to live merely for living or merely for the physical world benefits such as social success, and live under false pretenses with hopeless theory, and fall into unpleasant feelings. This will be the biggest reason why we can't create the expanded future. So those people who do not have courage to live with their own identities are more likely to fall into unpleasant feelings by themselves by bringing the theory of "nothing can start and nothing can be done without plans and schedules for the near future."

4-63. Spiritual consciousness and physical consciousness are paradox

Establishing Self-integration means that we direct physical desire, the relative objectivity, to the intention of the spiritual consciousness entity, the relative subjectivity, with SHINSEI as the common denominator according to the principle of dimensional integration, and then we direct Self-Enlightenment and spiritual evolution to a higher level of the spiritual dimension. That is, to direct the existing purpose and the existing value of the universe to the relative subjectivity of a higher spiritual dimension, as the cells are integrated to the tissue, the tissue is integrated to the organ, the organ is integrated to the body, the body is integrated to the spiritual consciousness entity, the "body mind" is integrated to the "soul mind," and the "soul mind" is integrated to SHINSEI, which is the common denominator of the universe, and completes to SHINSEI integrated life entity.

Based on the rule of "spirit is subjective and body is objective," the spiritual consciousness entity directs to release from the physical desire consciousness, which is the instinctive remaining consciousness by genetic domination, and acquire independency and freedom. The value that the spiritual consciousness entity directs for the spiritual world benefits, and the value that the desire consciousness of the body directs for the physical world benefits, are directed to the totally opposed purpose.

Human beings in the lower spiritual dimension and their

spiritual consciousness entity has no advanced differentiation and is immature, have the same personality and spirituality as chimpanzee bonobos, and have connoted undifferentiated sexual desire consciousness dominated by undifferentiated sexual impulse, and directed to sexual delusion and sexual disgrace, and look for peculiar sexual relationships with the same sex and opposite sex, being captured by physical pleasure, and would accomplish the poor personality formation by dependence on the worldly and material values.

Those in the lower spiritual dimension whose spiritual consciousness is young and immature, tend to prefer splendid and satiated lives, covering themselves with expensive materials such as high-class brands of clothing, high-class imported cars, and luxurious land and houses, and indulge in the cheap sense of superiority of Self-satisfaction and Self-intoxication. Those people are directed, unconditionally, to the mental state of the reverse vector to camouflage the poorness of the substance by the rule of balance.

4-64. The principal of dimensional integration of the cosmological love

When the spiritual consciousness entity becomes more mature and achieves spiritual evolution to higher level human beings, the classification toward the sexual desire consciousness becomes more notable, and the less they derive the undifferentiated sexual desire consciousness and sexual delusion, such as dirty sexual relationships, the more they are released from the physical world

Chapter Four ☆ The Conclusion

benefits, and live a simple life with a purpose. Such a person is unleashed from the material desire and the dominating desire, as the physical domination, and at last it will be possible to be released from the spell and the fate of the instinctive survival consciousnesses, and acquire freedom.

The principle of dimensional integration of the universe is *the things in the lower dimension are comprehended to the higher dimension, and the things in the higher dimension direct the things in the lower dimension to freedom and love in the higher level, and constantly work to integrate them.* In order to achieve spiritual evolution to a higher spiritual dimension, we should constantly aim for the way of life according to the rule of "spirit is subjective and body is objective," which integrates the body as the object, to the spiritual consciousness entity as the subject, by the way of life of PARAREVO.

However, the fated role and the theoretical framework on the earth star are occupied by how to make the soul, the spiritual consciousness entity, be subordinate to the body and direct it to inconvenience and unpleasant feelings, according to the rule of "body is subjective and spirit is objective." As evidence for that, most information, including the media, is broadcasting gossip, criticism and evaluation. Therefore, the spiritual consciousness entity is captured and detained by the body, and the principle of dimensional domination on the earth star is, *things in the higher dimension are detained by things in the lower dimension, and things in the lower dimension constantly work to direct and dominate things in the higher dimension, to inconvenience and unpleasant feelings of the lower level.*

Thus, verifying the history of evolution for human beings, from the universal dimension, the spiritual consciousness entity in the higher dimension has constantly been dominated by the body in the lower dimension, and tamed as the physical desire, throughout 3.8 billion years. All terrestrial lives from bacteria to human beings have common ecological behaviors based on the rule of "body is subjective and spirit is objective," according to the common desire consciousness based on the instinctive survival consciousnesses. Even though terrestrial lives on the earth are different shapes and sizes, the purposes for the ecological behaviors are to eat to complete the dietary desire consciousness for living, and also parenting and family support, which completes the sexual desire consciousness for the preservation of the species, so that we are not spending our life time for Self-Enlightenment and spiritual evolution.

As a result, human beings reign at the top of the food chain, and have built the social structure in which those who have strong desire dominate those who have less desire. In the deep consciousness of the people who want to reign at a company, gurus in the religious organizations, and the bureaucratic governing structure, always contain the dominating desire consciousness based on the undifferentiated sexual desire consciousness. Those people connote a huge disorder and defect toward love, in their spirituality formation history and the personality formation history, so that they have strong materialistic thought by physical domination, and the desire and the attachment toward the physical world benefits, politically and economically.

The physical domination life is *the physical desire dominating the spiritual consciousness entity and directing the consciousness to acquire excessive physical world benefits and evaluation from others, by enslavement.*

4-65. Establish Self-integrity by the way of PARAREVO life

The spiritual consciousness entity tamed by the body throughout 3.8 billion years on the earth, goes to the spiritual world after the disembodiment, but unfortunately stays in the intangible substantial world with the remaining inconvenience of this world by the habit of the consciousness, and it is not able to transcend the theoretical framework and value of the earth star, and will re-descend to this world again and again according to the rule of reincarnation. In order to complete the true existing purpose, you should direct the spiritual consciousness entity and the body to the relative subjectivity based on SHINSEI by the way of life of PARAREVO, and establish Self-integration by the relative original power integrated into the "Trinity" based on freedom and love.

For that, you have to aim to superintend yourself toward Self-evaluation based on truth, without other evaluation based on fact, and empathizing supposition and speculation. If you are the only human being on the earth, do you think there would be any evaluation of superiority or inferiority, happiness or unhappiness, rich or poor, moreover, relative evaluation of gratitude or dissatisfaction? Probably it would never happen. Because the channel of the spiritual dimension to connect the relative wave called human being does not exist, the relative original power which evaluates relatively would not derive.

Therefore, if you live by yourself, there is no meaning or significance to evaluate relatively like good and evil, superiority or inferiority, rich or poor, and the top or bottom, and logically, there will be no motivation to exercise unpleasant feelings. There is no way for living other than facing all kinds of environments, accepting as they are, unconditionally and totally, no matter if it rains and the wind blows, or it is cold or hot.

To establish Self-integrity is to direct truth, the presence of the consciousness based on SHINSEI, to the relative subjectivity in the higher dimension, constantly, and integrate it, and lead Self-Enlightenment and spiritual evolution toward the spiritual dimension of a higher level. People who live the way of life of PARAREVO draw the separation borderline between themselves and others strictly, toward the evaluation of others, finding the truth in the subjectivity and the cause of "I," and try Self-creation to direct the existing purpose and the existing value to the individual art in the higher spiritual dimension, by establishing Self-integrity.

The truth that can transcend the separation borderline between oneself and others is only the time when you open the path of feelings to create happiness based on love, and achieve Self-completion by directing yourself to the higher spiritual dimension. Otherwise, you will definitely fall into unpleasant feelings. In order to complete each existing purpose and existing value to the maximum, you should direct the individual purpose to the entire purpose in the higher dimension, open the path of feelings of love and happiness toward the higher spiritual dimension, and manifest the individual art with established Self-integrity. Therefore, based on *the principle of dimensional integration of love, the individual is the whole and*

Chapter Four ☆ The Conclusion

the whole is the individual. The integrated consciousness is an important concept.

When we observe the micro world in our body very carefully, the 60 trillion cells and the 110 trillion complex life assembly of microbes form the body of one human being. By completing each role and responsibility according to the existing purpose of each cell, the harmony and the order of the entire life will be formed, and by the perfect collaboration (completed co-existence and symbiosis), will be able to make the existence of one life entity. A brain cell completes the role and the responsibility according to the purpose of the brain cell. The heart cell completes the role and the responsibility according to the purpose of the heart cell. All cells of the organs and the entrails complete the role and the responsibility according to each existing purpose, such as the liver, the pancreas, the stomach, hands and feet, and they will complete the perfect collaboration of the entire life.

What would happen if a cell of the soles of the feet abandon the role and the responsibility and insist on being a brain cell? Or, what would happen if a cell of the liver wants to be a brain cell? All harmony and order will be destroyed and the existence of the entire life entities would be destroyed and disappear. The condition of distraction of this perfect collaboration system for the harmony and the order is called illness. For instance, a cancer cell destroys the harmony by acting Self-centered, continues to expand in disorder, and then invites the result to destroy the life entity itself.

Like this, the individual purpose is constantly directed and comprehended to the entire purpose, and the entire purpose constantly makes approaches to integrate by directing the individual purpose to the harmony and the order. When the mutual existing purposes are completed, the existing purpose of the whole and the individual is co-promoted, and forms the integrated perfect collaboration. In the cells and the organs of the human body the microscopic world, there is no superiority or inferiority, or discrimination between the top and the bottom. It always approaches to complete the individual role and responsibility to the entire purpose. Does the heart stop beating selfishly because it is tired? The heart works on to keep beating even if you have a myocardial infarction. Do the soles of the feet complain all the time? Like this, the cells for the tissues, the tissues for the organs, the organs for the entire purpose for the life entity to exist, since each of their benefits and values will be all equally restored and given to the entire cells by completing the role and responsibility, no matter if they are the brain cells or the cells of the soles of the feet.

In our human society, *the superiority or inferiority and discrimination at the top and the bottom exist as common place. Furthermore, in order to acquire excessive physical world benefits, and in order to taste a sense of superiority, people make an effort to create discrimination.* Is our presence as human beings beneath a single cell? In order to establish true Self-integrity, we should first of all establish the integrity between SHINSEI and the soul, and then integrate the soul and the body.

The principle of dimensional integration of love means *the individual purpose is given the role and the responsibility to further the entire purpose as a priority, and when it exists for the entire purpose of the higher dimension, the value of love is restored to all things equally, as well as sharing the place for the entire love, and the spiritual evolution becomes possible to the spiritual dimension of the entire purpose equally.* Universal love will be restored to the earth when the individual exists for the family, the family exists for the ethnic group, the ethnic group exists for the nation, the nation exists for the world, and the world exists for the earth. In order to establish true Self-integrity, we should form the harmony and the order, according to the vector directed toward the purpose of the higher dimension of the universe, and the subjective love, the verity of the individual entity called SHINSEI, and the objective happiness, the individual mental entity called "I," create the relative original power of love and happiness, and then will be integrated by the synergistic resonance wave. The path of feelings in which love is the subject and happiness is the object, is opened to the higher dimension, and integrates and manifests the internal world (the intangible substantial world) and the external world (the tangible substantial world) to a higher quality, by the creation of the individual art of a higher nature.

People who live the way of life of PARAREVO have the most interest in directing themselves to Self-Enlightenment and spiritual evolution, by directing the truth to the Self-integrity of the universal dimension, according to the principle of dimensional integration based on the rule of "spirit is subjective and body is objective," in order to graduate from the earth.

So, when the larger entire purpose in the higher dimension takes priority over the individual purpose, the existing purpose and the existing value for Self-Enlightenment and spiritual evolution will be completed, the entire freedom and love will be given to an individual, and it will become possible to achieve spiritual evolution by stepping up to a higher spiritual dimension. When each person clarifies the existing purpose to graduate from the earth star in the community called the earth, and completes the individual role and responsibility as the individual art perfectly, it will become possible to manifest the greater existing value of the universal dimension in the earth star.

4-66. SHINSEI is the receptor for everything in the universe

The rule of the creation power in the universe is that *all things existing in the universe contain SHINSEI as the common denominator, and make it possible to be relative by the spiritual network based on the channels of each spiritual dimension. This makes it possible to share the existence by the mechanism which derived the relative original power. This power is defined as the relative universal original power as a general term*. This relative universal original power and the whole creator world in the universe are forced to exist by directing all things to the objects and the effects, by the causal and the subjective power created by the relative original power based on the relative wave, which works in the lower dimension as the lower dimension and in the higher dimension as the higher dimension.

The existence of SHINSEI is not an exception. It exists directing to the relative subjectivity according to the principle of dimensional integration based on *the relative wave in the spiritual dimension and the rule of the relative original power*. SHINSEI, which is the spiritual presence in the intangible substantial world, and the universe, which is the material presence of the tangible substantial world, exist simultaneously and synchronically like two sides of same coin. This fundamental power itself, which derives by the relative original power between SHINSEI and the universe, is called the *"cosmological SHINSEI integration consciousness world."*

SHINSEI is not an incomparable and absolute presence, but a relative presence. SHINSEI has its own system to direct all functions of the universe to harmony and order by the sustainable mechanism in which SHINSEI can grow and exist eternally, by making it possible for dimensional integration of love, the subject, and happiness, the object, by the relative original power based on free love.

Therefore, SHINSEI achieves spiritual evolution by directing all things existing in the universe to a higher relative subjectivity, by accepting totally, whether good or evil, by *the principle of dimensional integration based on the rule of change by birth and re-birth.* The principle of dimensional integration based on the rule of change by birth and re-birth is the mechanism and the system by which the "soul mind" itself achieves spiritual evolution to a higher spiritual dimension, by changing and re-birthing the "body mind." This rule and the principle form the fundamental theoretical framework of the PARAREVO theory, and are the core equations for spiritual evolution.

4-67. SHINSEI is the receptor for everything of the entire personality

We human beings are the analogous entity and the epitome of

the universe, contain SHINSEI, and are possible to exist by the same system as the universe. The spiritual consciousness and the physical body are also possible to exist by the life power derived by the relative original power with SHINSEI. Since SHINSEI is the receptor for everything of our entire personality, and the source of power which is possible to be relative to the entire dimension, it derives the relative original power to both the "soul mind" and the "body mind." We evoke the consciousness and make the words and the deeds based on the motivation of good and evil, so according to this rule, *the existence of the consciousness based on SHINSEI, whether the "soul mind" or "body mind," is the "truth,"* which is proven cosmologically.

By the total acceptance of SHINSEI, the existence of the spiritual consciousness entity and the body are also accepted and directed to the relative subjectivity according to the principle of dimensional integration of love, and will become possible to complete Self-Enlightenment and spiritual evolution step by step, with the Self-integrity to accept the poor environment and the ONSHU of the lower dimension totally, just like SHINSEI itself accepts everything unconditionally

Integrating oneself to SHINSEI is explained as follows. *SHINSEI is the verity of the individual entity containing the relative original power, which exists in the slight fluctuation of imperfection within opposite things based on the rule of entropy relativity, and accepts the intention of the soul, the relative subjectivity, and the intention of the body, the relative objectivity, unconditionally and totally, making oneself present and alive without exhausting and emphasizing feelings toward anything.*

Therefore, SHINSEI in ourselves never interferes or intervenes toward the decision we made based on the rule of freedom, and leaves all things to our Self-responsibility.

4-68. The importance of Logos and the concept of way of life

Logos (words: the spirit of language) have an origin. There is always a truth which corroborates the consciousness for the background of why and how the logos began, and as a fact of the result based on the motivation; they were born as tangible words. Therefore, logos exist as the first tangible sound for the voice of intangible consciousness.

Logos are the voice of the consciousness and a tool for living. Tools are nothing but tools. They could be an offensive weapon of Self-injury if you misuse them. Even though we have freedom of speech, words should always be accompanied with responsibility. There is always somebody who says irresponsible things, such as "you are so lucky because…" or "this is the best." It is the same as people chanting Buddhism sutra, praying words in Christianity or Islamic for saving yourself or going to Heaven or awaking yourself. If we are able to achieve Self-completion when we just chant the praying words, we don't need to make the Self-effort to do things, so we lose all meaning and significance to make the effort. Recently, because words are in disorder, there are many religious people and people in spiritual groups who tell lies unconcernedly with the hypocrisy of Self-satisfaction by inciting fear of the future.

Since people who live the way of life of PARAREVO carry through an undeniable existentialism, they will never be immersed in Self-satisfaction and Self-intoxication by fantasying like chanting prayer words or do false meditation. If they have such free time, they practice existential love to love others close to them, like their neighbors and family by doing their best with all their heart and mind in order to *release their own ONSHU by loving the ONSHU.*

The time axis called the past and the future is created by the concept of the human brain, like a delusion. The time axis was merely made by the movement of the sun and the moon which simply experiences the changing the seasons in the nature world. If the world would be only darkness or light eternally, the concept of the time axis would not have been produced. Therefore, there is no time and calendar existing in the universe. The zero time period of every moment called *the Now* only exists in digital. If you are enjoying the fantasy world by merely participating in a meditation meeting or chanting praying words, etc., it is ok, however, if you live the present by believing the future, it is not so different from a schizophrenic who suffered from mental disorders with delusions and auditory hallucinations, you are living by things which do not exist.

The existing purpose and the existing value in this world are nothing more than to train our soul and mind to achieve Self-Enlightenment and accomplish spiritual evolution to a higher spiritual dimension, in order to prepare for the life in the spiritual world of the universe. Evidently, depravity of human beings and their "body mind" seem that *it is the desire to achieve Self-realization easily and comfortably.* For example, we can devote ourselves to investment business in stocks or gambling in casinos

Chapter Four ☆ The Conclusion

seeking unearned income, or get ourselves into a network business seeking easy income.

If we win the lottery, is it really a lucky life? Even if we are satisfied economically, there is no meaning if we fall into personality destruction with poor mind. In fact, many people who won the lottery had changed their personality from before and fallen into an arrogant and lazy life. Those who are considered successful people in this life are somewhat arrogant, and proud of their autocratic management, so I feel the poorness and ugliness of their mind, and cannot possibly think that with their personality they are humble and modest.

I would say that the spiritual wave entities of greedy, malicious, and poor spirit, Self-trapped in this world, exist behind those who induce depravity and the "body mind" of human beings by saying that "it is possible to make the Self-materialization easily and comfortably." People who, like *Satan and demons* pretend to be good like angels of the light, make enjoying the "body mind" and the depravity of human beings directing them toward the physical world benefits, promote all techniques to induce worldly desires, behave persuasively and gently, and guide to the direction of corruption by keeping the consciousness away from the true purpose of life.

So, do not seek the excessive Self-realization toward the future, but try to make Self-completion to accept the present by gratitude and happiness. There is no such thing as a magic word. A magic word is undoubtedly the devil's word which is the spirit of language of demons and confuses the world. Basically you can say anything because you have freedom of speech; however, you have to take responsibility when your words cause fear and anxiety, or laziness in people.

People who live the way of PARAREVO understand clearly about logos. The existence of the consciousness based on SHINSEI is the only truth, and all other things are only fact, or supposition and speculation. Even sciences exist in the world of supposition and speculation.

Logos are set free from the truth of the consciousness and carried in the distance as sound (fact). So, untruth, fabrication and deception occur in the process from truth to fact. For example, you can say the words which are totally opposite from what you think by hiding your uncomfortable feelings, but you are not able to deceive your consciousness. Since the words easily create untruth, fabrication, and deception, they never reach to the truth. *It is because words are the tool for the consciousness and the communication tool in the lower dimension, which were born from the rule of "body is subjective and spirit is objective," due to the presence of the body.*

Since those who live the way of life of PARAREVO *always try to open the path of the feelings by directing the object to happiness with the subject of love,* they face truth with the vital wave (aura) and the life wave (soma) as a clue, and try to work for mental interchange beyond languages. Words are a hindrance causing untruth, fabrication, and deception. When the PARAREVO people make a commitment with truth, they do not need words at all because they consider the wave interchange as a clue. They perceive the vital wave and the life wave immediately, and conduct unconsciously the wave interchange and emotional interchange by adapting to the spiritual dimension of the other person, naturally. The reason they aim for such a way of life is that the existing purpose and the

Chapter Four ☆ The Conclusion

existing value of this world are preparation for the spiritual life, and *words do not exist in the spiritual world where the body does not exist.*

Since, in the spiritual world, we human beings are not able to hide the spiritual consciousness entity by covering it with the body, because things we think and feel with the consciousness are brought to others immediately. *The spiritual world is the place where there is no fact and only truth exists.*

4-69. All things necessary have to be good

Your assignments in this life will happen no matter what you do, even if you practice meditation or recite the Buddhist scriptures, pray to God, or anything else. It happens inevitably, but not accidentally. Your life is directed by the cause, the problem, and the assignment, which you have drawn in the spiritual world by yourself and, the responsibility of your assignment of your life is Self-evaluated by the method of points subtracted from your life, against your Self-management by Self-determination and Self-completion by Self-responsibility. Therefore, it doesn't matter if you are lucky or unlucky, the fact which should happen will happen inevitably, and things which should become real will become real. By the same token, things which should not happen will not happen, and things should not become real will not become real.

People who have illusions of the phenomenon, believing it happened as lucky by chance, have a strong tendency to assume things and the habit of delusional day-dreaming. Leaders of spiritual groups and gurus of religious groups have schizophrenic tendencies with day-dreaming and myth-mania. And, by the relative wave in the spiritual dimension and the rule of the relative original power, those who have similar tendencies have strong and wrong assumption, create groups and organizations with unquestioning belief and fanaticism by Self-trapping, according to the rule of group. Since gurus, leaders of spiritual groups and some mediums would have shouldered serious psychogenic trauma in their personality formation history, and the condition of their soul and body are in a big fluctuation of imperfection, instead of in a slight fluctuation of imperfection, there is a large crack and gap between the soul and the body, and their condition makes it easy to invite the bad spirits and malicious spirits in the lower dimension through the chakras.

Lucky or unlucky is the relative evaluation from others, so you should establish Self-integrity by directing arrows to yourself, as you are the only one existing on the earth. And if you are the only one on the earth, evaluations such as superiority or inferiority, happiness or unhappiness, wealth or poverty, or lucky or unlucky do not exist, moreover, they do not have any meaning or significance for living. So, there is no other way but to face to all environments, and live with the Self-responsibility to accept everything unconditionally and totally.

Establishing Self-integrity means to direct the arrows of the consciousness always toward oneself, not to emit feelings or empathize toward the evaluation from others at all, and no matter what happens in life, interpret phenomena as fact, direct them to the relative subjectivity by truth, and accept them unconditionally. Since we are the life entity with a fate of the death of the body anyway, if we establish the real view of life and death by directing

Chapter Four ☆ The Conclusion

ourselves to truth of the higher spiritual dimension, no matter how big the problems are in this life, the hurdle will become lower and, the assignments and the responsibility we need to bear will become smaller.

The most important truth in life is Self-evaluation toward Self-determination based on SHINSEI integration consciousness, in how we *accept things which might happen in life as they are, unconditionally and totally with gratitude and happiness,* with the concept of *necessary things have to be good.*

4-70. True Self-realization is unconditional Self-completion

The purpose of life in this world is only for the spiritual benefits to be sublimated to the eternal spiritual world after graduating from the earth star not for the benefits for this world to gain status, honor, and property.

The benefits for this world are the method of subtracting points from your life against the responsibility of your assignments, and the benefits for the spiritual world are the method of adding points to your life for the responsibility of assignments. Since the benefits for the spiritual world are the method of adding points, it is only adding for the evaluation toward truth, but not the evaluation toward fact. And the level of the spiritual dimension is determined by the offset of the volume of exercises between the "body mind" and the "soul mind."

Your role and the responsibility of life are to make the best Self-effort for Self-completion with *the unconditional acceptance of everything* toward your assignment in this world. Therefore, even if you practice a success philosophy very hard for your dream and wish, if you do not have assignment and responsibility for them, you will never fulfill them as your Self-realization.

Many people are not able to make their wish come true easily, such as if they want to go to a specific place but will never be able to go. Why is that? All results are guided and become possible to turn into reality by the relative original power. So, the reason they cannot go is because they are not receiving an invitation from the place they would like to go. The thought of mutual direction, for instance, "I would like to go to Hawaii, so, Hawaii should come to me," corresponds relatively, then finally the consciousness is evoked by the relative original power, and the fact to go to Hawaii will be manifested based on the motivation. Those people can't go to Hawaii even though they want to, because Hawaii is not inviting them yet.

As a matter of course, the reason you are not able to make Self-realization is because you have not received an invitation from the result of Self-realization. And the reason, for instance, why you are not able to enter the university you want, why you are not able to obtain a position with a firm where you would like to work, or why you are not able to accomplish the Self-realization you would like, no matter how hard you try, is because the relativity of mutual direction with your assignment and the responsibility do not exist.

No matter how hard you try to gain the physical world benefits and direct the motivation toward them, if the path between the cause and the effect, according to each spiritual dimension, is not open in the spiritual world, the relative original power based on

Chapter Four ☆ The Conclusion

truth would not derive, so the act and the result as fact based on the exercise of the consciousness and the motivation would not be fulfilled as Self-realization. If you are able to materialize the things you are wishing for unilaterally, as the one way method, nobody will have a hard time in this world. However, the rule of the universe is not the one-way method; instead, the cause and the effect are interactive method of mutual direction. In some spiritual groups, there is a tendency to believe that if you are conscious of things they would manifest, however, that will never happen.

Since the physical world benefits are the method of subtracting points, the results in the lower dimension are accomplished easily without any effort, however, the benefits for the spiritual world are the method of adding points, so the results in the higher dimension would never be accomplished easily in the category of merely Self-efforts in the temporal world. Since things which do not exist in the spiritual world are not able to manifest in the real world, based on the rule of "spirit is subjective and body is objective," if you want to achieve Self-realization in this world such as wishes, goals, hopes and dreams of life, you should direct your life every day toward the relative subjectivity of the higher spiritual dimension, aim the way of life based on truth of the higher dimension, accumulate the spiritual achievements in the spiritual world which is the world of cause, and then complete them in this world as the world of result.

When you can live the way of life of PARAREVO, you can save unnecessary Self-effort in this world, can dissolve the negative legacy, and as a result, you can achieve the Self-realization in this world and direct the benefits of the spiritual world with which you can obtain true freedom, as the positive legacy, and it suggests the possibility of Self-completion in the spiritual world of the universe. If you only have a small dream, you only recite "be lucky and Glory to the Sutra" with *the hypocrisy of Self-satisfaction and narcissism.* However, if you aim for Self-Enlightenment and spiritual evolution, you should practice the way of life *to achieve Self-completion with gratitude and happiness, by accepting everyday life unconditionally and totally based on love, with deep affection and Self-sacrifice.* This kind of life becomes a cornerstone, and as a result, Self-realization and Self-completion will become possible quickly and certainly.

4-71. The way of PARAREVO life makes your entire life "truly lucky"

There are countless people in the world who have practiced philosophy of success thoroughly, however, how many persons can succeed by the practice of philosophy of success? Probably, those who did not succeed were the majority. Being lucky or unlucky is the relative evaluation of the fact in the phenomenon, but it is not the subjective evaluation of truth which one has decided by himself/herself.

Whether it is the phenomenon of being lucky or unlucky, it is the relative evaluation with the excessive physical world benefits as the center, and the evaluation from others has no meaning and significance for one self. The evaluation as being "blessed" and/or lucky will be a totally different concept by whether it is the benefits and values of the physical world or the benefits for the spiritual world. If you have the former view of value, those who obtained status, reputation, and property are the ones who are fortunate and

Chapter Four ☆ The Conclusion

lucky. With such a theory, people like Jesus and Mahatma Gandhi would be the symbolic beings who are unfortunate or unlucky.

Being fortunate or unfortunate, lucky or unlucky based on truth depends on the place where the presence of the consciousness of that person is, but it is not in the evaluation from others or the worldly values based on fact. *We must distinguish purpose and aim. Purpose is Self-completion, which the all human beings hold equally, in order to graduate from the earth star, and aim is the Self-realization, which is up to each individual.*

People who live the way of PARAREVO consider that the greatest theme for life is *the purpose of Self-completion rather than the aim of Self-realization.* So, they do not live a worldly way of life in which people have the anxiety and fear of losing whatever they gained and at the same time are incited to further desire and become slaves of endless desire, even though they achieve Self-realization based on the excessive physical world benefits.

The PARAREVO people try to complete their life for the spiritual world benefits which achieve Self-completion based on spiritual evolution, and manifest the individual art of freedom and love which they do not lose, eternally. Therefore, they are never trapped in the relative evaluation of superiority or inferiority, or the acquisition for evaluation from others such as *winners or habitual winners,* never expel or empathize emotions, but make the maximum Self-effort for Self-completion by accepting as they are, unconditionally and totally, with gratitude and happiness, even if they are in tragic conditions and others sympathized with them.

The most important thing in life is to achieve Self-completion by your own responsibility, with the determination of the will to *accept as they are, unconditionally and totally, with gratitude and happiness no matter what happened.* If you do so, it means that you will live a "truly lucky" life, throughout the lifetime as your Self-evaluation. The practice for *the way of life of PARAREVO* is the best way to acquire the power of will to accept everything as it is, unconditionally and totally with gratitude and happiness, by surpassing and transcending with love as strength for the spiritual consciousness entity and it is the best equation for Self-Enlightenment and spiritual evolution.

Since the system to achieve Self-Enlightenment and spiritual evolution is internalized by the mechanism to create happiness together with yourself and others, by acting with love as the motivation toward all ONSHU, the equation for spiritual evolution is nothing more than practicing the way of life of PARAREVO *to release your own ONSHU by loving the ONSHU.*

4-72. The rule of freedom is the fundamental rule of the universe

The rule of freedom is the fundamental rule of the universe, and it precedes the rule of love. *You can love with or without freedom, however, because you have love does not necessarily mean you have freedom. Without the rule of freedom, equality, possibility and sustainability will be lost.*

Our presence is accepted unconditionally and totally by *existing SHINSEI, which is inside us,* and we are forced to exist by *the truth that we are alive in the Now,* which is by the relative original power between SHINSEI and the spiritual consciousness entity, and the

Chapter Four ☆ The Conclusion

fact that we live in the Now, by the relative original power between the spiritual consciousness entity and the body.

The mechanism of the universe is always directed to a higher dimension. For instance, elementary particles are directed to atoms, atoms to molecules, molecules to cells, cells to organs, and organs are directed to the whole body systems. So individuals are directed to the whole, expanding their love. Even the human body follows this rule, because we human beings are the epitome of the universe, so we exist by the mechanism, the same as the universe. We are allowed to live by the truth and live with the fact, which is also the same rule of the universe. The universe is completed in the truth and the fact for which the whole universe is alive, and lives with the present by *the existing SHINSEI which is in the universe,* by being accepted in the Now, unconditionally and totally.

Thus, *SHINSEI of the universe and SHINSEI of the individual exist as the common denominator, and direct the consciousness to the higher level based on the common intention.* It could be said that both exist with the same root and spirit. Each spiritual dimension is determined by the individual mental entity, which exists as the individual molecule, and is dimensionally integrated by the verity of the individual entity, which is SHINSEI of the universe, and is forced to exist by being directed to the spiritual dimension of the higher level. So, we can say that "we are the perfect existence." It is just a matter of whether we understand it or not. If the existing religions had understood this, I have no doubt that we would not have built such miserable history by the Self-righteous theory of good and evil and the theory of superiority or inferiority.

There is only one reason for all things existing in the entire universe. That is to open the path of the feelings in both directions, with the feeling of love as the subject and the feeling of happiness as the object, so the existing purpose and the value are directed and integrated to the higher level by the relative original power of love and happiness. *SHINSEI has exercised the subjective consciousness, called the impulsive feeling of love, which would like to obtain happiness, so it has been forced to create the bipolar existence of the universe, based on the motivation to obtain the object for happiness.* This rule of the creation of the original power in the universe is called *the rule of the relative original power of love and happiness.* It is because love and happiness direct the freest relativity, which can be both the subject and the object.

SHINSEI of the universe is the cause of love, and since the universe exists synchronically and simultaneously as the result of happiness, SHINSEI is the cause of my own love and "I" exist synchronically and simultaneously as the result of happiness. For the relationship between SHINSEI and the individual, the mind and the spirit which is the personality of the individual spirit, and the true spirit which is the spirituality of the universal spirit, manifest as the individual art by *the relative original power based on the mind and the spirit,* by the path of the feelings like parent-child relationship, which is love as the subject and happiness as the object.

4-73. SHINSEI itself evolves by the rule of freedom

If SHINSEI and "I" are connected with the feeling like parent-child, at which moment does SHINSEI obtain the real happiness?

Chapter Four ☆ The Conclusion

Basically, the moment the parents feel happiness toward their children is the moment when the children surpass and transcend the parents, based on freedom and love, and achieve greater and more excellent growth than the parents. In other words, *the moment when the children transcend the parents is the greatest moment of happiness.* At that moment, the subject of love and the object of happiness are dimensionally integrated to the spiritual dimension in the higher level, by the rule of change by birth and re-birth, creating the mechanism to be able to grow eternally, and complete the system, directing to evolution.

Naturally, we can say the same thing for the relationship between SHINSEI and the spiritual consciousness entity. Our spiritual consciousness entity is directed to the spiritual dimension of the higher level by SHINSEI, and when it transcends SHINSEI, SHINSEI will complete to the regeneration of SHINSEI and the soul of new higher dimension synchronically and simultaneously, by *the principle of dimensional integration by the rule of change by birth and re-birth.*

Like this, SHINSEI is not the peerless and the absolute completed existence. SHINSEI itself contains the possibility to evolve by directing to the relative subjectivity by being the relative existence of the slight fluctuation of imperfection, and thus the generation and the development for the entire universe is directed. By this system, it is possible for SHINSEI itself to keep growing eternally, and SHINSEI and the spiritual consciousness entity complete the spiritual pair system which they created as the mutual aid system for spiritual evolution, by the principle of dimensional integration based on the rule of change by birth and re-birth.

The indispensable rule of the universe, in order to complete this mechanism and the system perfectly, is *the rule of freedom*. Therefore, *freedom has the greatest priority, and is the SHINSEI integration consciousness world which is carried through by the principle of nonaggression and nonintervention, which nobody can violate.*

4-74. The 21st century is the end of monotheism

If SHINSEI was defined as the unique and the absolute completed presence of God of the universe and defined as the unilateral creator which had created all things in the universe with the theoretical framework and the value as monotheism, it is not possible to overcome the absolute creator, and the size of the universe should be fixed. If so, the universe would be unified and dominated by the absolute being, God, and would become the extremely inconvenient existence in the framework of God. And, God itself is not able to grow, so God will be the saddest presence in the universe.

Since the generation and the development become possible to sustain due to the slight fluctuation of imperfection, creativity, possibility, and sustainability will be lost in the perfection. We do connote our "body mind" and "soul mind" inside of us. When this "body mind" is exercised, the "soul mind" also exercises to surpass it, so it will be possible for us to achieve spiritual evolution to a new stage. So, if freedom and love would never function by *the one-way method,* the entropy inside the universe would increase, keep expanding, and soon destroy the universe itself like a balloon expands and bursts, and invites the result for Self-destruction.

Was there any meaning or significance for God to take the trouble to create things to be Self-destroyed? If such a fact exists, the universe would invite the struggle and the destruction together with the increase of entropy, and would not already exist. Although this is about the earth star, the concept of monotheism in which God is the unique and the absolute existence, such as in Judaism, Islam and Christianity, is bipolarized by the theory of good and evil and becomes Self-righteous with the consciousness exercised unconditionally by being exclusive of each other and trying to drive each other out, is inevitably directed to the struggle theory of good and evil, and reaches to the fight and the destruction. As a result, it has invited religious struggles many times in history and developed into religious wars, and still now has continued in the world.

In the 21st century, based on the PARAREVO theory, the earth will be either forced to invite the end of the monotheism, or collapse and Self-destruct by religious terrorism with the threat of nuclear war by monotheism.

4-75. The rule of freedom based on Self-responsibility

The universe manifests the universal art called the creation of happiness, by the integrative love between the verity of the individual entity called SHINSEI and the individual mental entity called the relative creator world.

By this exercise of the mental and spiritual consciousness, the universe transcends all things in the material world, opens the path of inner feelings to a higher level and creates the universal art of the higher dimension by mutual aid, and still continues to grow even now. Therefore, according to this system, it manifests the individual art called the creation of happiness, by the integration of relative love between SHINSEI, the verity of the individual entity, and "I," the individual mental entity, opens the path of inner feelings by transcending the physical senses by the exercises of the mental and spiritual consciousness, creates the life entity in the higher spiritual dimension by helping each other, and continues to evolve throughout history.

We need the rule of freedom to complete this system. If the parents create everything and form them as the absolute existence, the children would lose the opportunity to grow. When the parents give freedom to their children, children are able to grow by transcending the parents, and at the same time, the parents obtain the opportunity to grow as well.

SHINSEI is not going to interfere, mediate, or intervene at all toward all things existing in the universe, according to the principle of nonaggression and nonintervention, in order to guarantee the rule of freedom. Because it will violate the most fundamental rule of freedom and it will lose the equality, possibility, and sustainability, and moreover, it loses the existing purpose and the existing value and the possibility for each to grow, and end up losing its own existence. *The rule of freedom is the source of the creation of love and happiness by the rule of the fundamental relative universal original power of the universe, and the most important rule to direct all things to the generation and the development equally and eternally, with SHINSEI as the common denominator.* Therefore, *nobody can invade or take one`s free intention by force.*

Even if you are placed in a poor environment based on fact and

Chapter Four ☆ The Conclusion

somebody drives you to death, nobody can invade and take your freedom which is the root of your intention based on truth and love. Everybody is given the use of the rule of freedom to transcend the physical domination and direct the intention to accept as they are, unconditionally and totally, with gratitude and happiness, by the way of life of PARAREVO. In this sense, *our spiritual consciousness entity is actually the completely free presence which has transcended the body since we were born to this world.*

However, since the moment the primitive life entity was born on the earth star, the soul has been dominated by the instinctive survival consciousnesses and has continued shouldering the dietary desire and the sexual desire as a fate. In the long history of 3.8 billion years, the soul, the spiritual consciousness entity, has continuously been dominated by the five physical senses and tamed by the genetic domination by the instinctive survival consciousnesses, and, as a prisoner being dressed in a prison uniform called the body, continued the inconvenient history.

In our body, there is sense of pain when we get sick or injured, however, in SHINSEI and the spiritual consciousness entity, pain does not exist because they transcend the physical senses. There is no unhealthy disease or unhappiness, even the phenomenon of death does not exist by the rule of "the attainment of the spiritual being during life."

In the physical consciousnesses, there are five senses; touch, sight, hearing, taste, and smell. Also we have another sense for the spiritual consciousness entity, which is sensitivity and inner feelings, which exists in a higher level than the five senses. This sense always makes one be frightened of pain, which is the physical senses of the lower dimension, and anxiety and fear of death, and has continued to enslave the way of life by being dominated, by anxiety and fear, and afraid of unhappiness, in which we had no choice but to be subordinated to the body.

The habit of physical domination has made the spiritual consciousness entity inconvenient and captive in the body. There are many people who have been dominated by excessive physical world benefits and are living by the acquisition competition for evaluation from others. It is exactly the same as the consciousness being restricted by a preconceived concept, like a cage. In that case, we will never be released from the earth star. Therefore, in order to obtain true freedom we should always aim to practice the way of life of PARAREVO for release from physical domination.

4-76. The rule of the relative field based on love

The things existing in the universe, inevitably, have the existing purpose. So, every single thing has the role and the responsibility to complete the existing purpose. In order to share each existing value by opening the path of feelings of love and happiness to the higher dimension based on the rule of the relative field, it will be possible to manifest the maximum existing purpose and value, and complete them.

Does your right hand exist for your right hand? When a prickle sticks in your right hand, is the right hand able to pull the prickle out by itself? Probably it is impossible. You must use your left hand to pull out the prickle in the right hand. In other words, the right hand is useless for the right hand itself. Eyes do not exist for eyes,

Chapter Four ☆ The Conclusion

feet do not exist for feet, the liver does not exist for the liver, and the stomach does not exist for the stomach. So, when we look around, we find that nothing exists for itself.

The principle of the integration of love in the universe is that *things in the lower dimension are comprehended to things in the higher dimension, and things in the higher dimension always work to integrate with things in the lower dimension to free direction of the higher level.* Based on this principle of integration of love, we can understand the existing purpose of the body, in which the cell exists for the tissue, the tissue exists for the organs, the organs exist for the entire body, moreover, the body exists for the spiritual consciousness entity, the spiritual consciousness entity exists for SHINSEI, and SHINSEI exists for the universe. Like this, the individual purpose is directed toward the entire purpose, always works to share the existing value for the entire purpose, and the entire purpose works to restore and give the existing purpose to the individual.

When the individual purpose exists to further entire purpose as priority, it will be possible for the individual purpose to share the entire value. Because the consciousness and the motivation of SHINSEI as the starting point of the creation of the universe, *SHINSEI exercises the subjective consciousness, called the impulse of love which wanted to obtain happiness and was forced to create and exist the universe based on the motivation that it wanted to obtain the object of happiness.*

All things existing in the universe contain *the relative universal original power,* which is the entire purpose and the impulsive original power of the creation of love that wants to receive happiness, and they contain *the universal original power,* which is the power generated by individuals and directed toward love, based on the rule of "individual is whole, whole is individual." *The relative universal original power* of universal love and *the universal original power* of individual happiness are making resonance by connecting with each other relatively, and working to open the path of inner feelings of love and happiness toward the higher level.

For all things existing in the universe, no matter which dimension they are in, the existing purpose and the existing value is based on love, and *nothing exists for itself.* Even if we get a disease, have an accident or are unhappy, they exist in order for us to realize something essential. Fundamentally, they connote the motivation of love, and exist by being directed to the greater entire purpose. Even though we have a life of penance and hardship, or trials and tribulations, it will be possible for us to complete spiritual evolution toward the higher spiritual dimension when we overcome the conditions by true love and convert it to happiness.

Therefore, *in the universe, nothing exists for Self-centeredness, and nothing exists at all without being based on love.*

4-77. Individual mental entities manifest individual art

Individuality is expressed as an art toward everything, and moreover, should be completed to happiness based on freedom and love. Since art has no limitation and keeps an unlimited creation power, the sustainable individual art is opened to a higher spiritual dimension with the path of inner feelings called love and happiness, and manifests, eternally.

Chapter Four ☆ The Conclusion

Once each person manifests his/her own individual art on the earth and starts enjoying it, it will be possible for human beings to build the world of true co-existence, mutual prosperity, and symbiosis. Because the world of the spiritual consciousness entity, the intangible substantial world, is the world of intangible substantial art in where the subjective love of SHINSEI, the verity of the individual entity, and the objective happiness of the soul, the individual mental entity, are expressed as the sensitivity and inner feelings of the individual art, and are the harmony of love. It will be inevitable for one to find the individuality of one's own self in order to evolve the spiritual consciousness entity and enjoy the intangible substantial world.

To find your own individuality means to discover your own self and it is essential for your life since the individuality will become an important guide and a compass for your life. Finding your own individuality means finding something you really like. Individuality is the essential presence, which can be called a natural talent given to that person, and to manifest the individuality means to bring out the potential ability and talent given to that person. *"Devoting oneself to one's favorite thing by pouring in all energies"* means that the individuality can be a driving force to transcend the physical desire of the instinctive survival consciousnesses, based on love, and directs to happiness.

It will make a big difference for that person to live a precious and irreplaceable life, whether or not he/she has something to transcend the physical domination and live with motivation in life by love and happiness of the soul. When we devote ourselves to something we really like, it is the most beautiful and sparkling moment for human beings, and that is the moment we find the great partner with which we can enjoy life together as the individual art. In such an occasion, it is possible to make Self-completion of the best love collaboration in the sensitivity and inner feelings to sympathize with each other by integrating all things involved with love and happiness.

However, since the terrestrial lives, from bacteria to human beings, have the common ecological behavior according to the common desire consciousness based on the instinctive survival consciousnesses, we actually are not able to live a way of life with a great deal of personality by giving ourselves up for the existing social system, are superintended by the worldly theoretical framework and value, are absorbed in the physical world benefits for life and preservation of the species, so we select the life we do not want. As a result, since those who do not have courage to live with their individuality live by reversing life against their potential natural talent and ability, and increase trouble and anxiety more than necessary with conflict and unpleasant feelings, and direct to a life with less achievement.

Those who do not have any fulfillment in life, but only unpleasant feelings without gratitude and happiness, make the passive and momentary life compromise by the hopeless theory, and do not understand even their own individuality and their Self-realization, will die out like a dead tree when they reach their old age. Even though they made the Self-determination to spend a momentary life, they do not have Self-responsibility toward courage and belief to obtain freedom by being independent, with the dependent life of shifting the responsibility with many excuses. There is a tendency that those people who lose a fortune in life and fall victim to Self-destruction by the chain of unhappiness will increase more and more.

4-78. Individual subjectivity makes individual art sustainable

What shall we do in order to live with the individual art as the subject? We must clarify the existing purpose and the existing value of our own life, make our own individuality the priority, have courage to give up work we do not like, and have the belief to choose a life's work which we really like.

If you do not have the courage and belief to live with the individuality as the subject, make Self-escape by the hopeless theory, preserve the worldly vested interests which you have built, and decide for yourself to be dependent on others such as a company, you should not fall into unpleasant feelings, but should accept as they are unconditionally and totally with gratitude and happiness by shouldering Self-responsibility. Those who do not have courage to live with the individuality have a tendency to have unpleasant feelings such as complaint, dissatisfaction, and insufficiency, and live their precious life for social success without any emotion, gratitude, impression, and happiness, make criticism against their superiors and company with unpleasant feelings, live the life of Self-injury by Self-hatred and Self-denial, and end up falling into Self-destruction.

Even in the relationship between married couples, women pretend to be happy by the economic ties, replace their marriage with *the hopeless theory* because of the position of *wife,* and make an irreplaceable life meaningless, insignificant, and momentary. If the *wife* would like to live with Self-completion without regrets, she must not depend on the economy of her husband, and have the courage and belief to obtain freedom by being independent.

The courage and conviction to live with the individual entity as the subject will lead the life to the individual art, make gratitude and happiness sustainable, and make it possible to manifest the individual art to the higher dimension by opening the door to good fortune. The way of life of PARAREVO, in which we live with the individual entity as the subject, gives value to your life and makes it possible for co-existence, mutual prosperity, and symbiosis.

If a person who likes fish and loves fishing becomes a fisherman, he will not do excessive fishing for economic supremacy and deplete and destroy the marine resources. Those fishermen will surly protect the marine resources and the natural environment, love the ocean and rivers, constantly form co-existence, mutual prosperity, and symbiosis, and while developing the harmony and the order of the natural world to the higher dimension, they will be involved in the fishing industry gently with love, and promote the existing value by giving the values toward the fishing industry to the whole nation. By the same token, if a person who loves plants and cultivation becomes involved in agriculture, he/she will develop functional agricultural technology focusing on natural farming rather than relying on pesticides and chemical fertilizers. That kind of person has a profound love of the earth, will form co-existence, mutual prosperity, and symbiosis, become united with nature and the earth by communicating with crops, and it will become more possible to promote a higher level of vegetables and give the value

Chapter Four ☆ The Conclusion

to the whole nation.

Words of wisdom since old times, say that "one will do the best at what one likes." Why is that? It is because it is based on the principle of love integration of the universe. Invisible influence of the universe is *things in the lower dimension are comprehended to things in the higher dimension, and things in the higher dimension always aim to integrate things in the lower dimension to higher level of freedom.* When you do things you like, the invisible relative influence from the universe will work and wisdom and intelligence will be given, and it will be possible to invoke the innovative ideas and inventions and the power of your potential gift. The eminent historical scientists and inventors were given the ultimate wisdom and the discovery of the innovative ideas from the universe, when they were immersed in things they liked.

Everybody will be given the wisdom and the intelligence from the universe unconditionally, if they put love into something they really like according to their own individuality, and concentrate on the creation of happiness, not being dominated by the excessive physical world benefits and the relative evaluation beyond the instinctive survival consciousnesses and carry out the existing purpose together for the individual purpose and the entire purpose, and then it will become possible to manifest the individual art by directing the existing value to the higher level.

4-79. Individual subjectivity releases the past practice of causality

In Japan, the traditional custom of the causality of many human societies is that a child in a political family would be a politician, a child of an actor became an actor, a son of a farmer would be a farmer even though he did not want to, a son of a fisherman became a fisherman even though he would not like it, and so on. I feel like they selected their precious and irreplaceable life by simply following the custom without any purpose, by *the hopeless theory,* in some kind of succession of the parents and the social flow. In such a society with no identity of the individual, creativity, artistry, and all other possibilities will be completely lost, so that we only form a Self-injurious society by Self-hatred and Self-denial, bury ourselves in a dull and uninteresting life, without any tenderness because of the competition society, and accumulating stress by suspicions and fear.

Since the individuality is a seed sowed in the spiritual consciousness entity, we are able to make that seed put forth buds and cherish it and allow it to open to a beautiful flower. When each person achieves Self-discovery for the favorite individuality, and lives a life to raise that individuality, the entire society will be full of vitality, and it will be possible to form a sustainable artistic, creative and expanding society, and make the harmony and the order of the entire society toward the higher dimension.

4-80. Individual subjectivity builds global collaboration

The majority of people, whose belief is based on the theoretical framework of the earth dimension, would say that if everybody does whatever they want, the harmony and the order of the society could

Chapter Four ☆ The Conclusion

not form. However, that is not true.

Even the mechanism of the infinite universe, from each of a fixed star, planet, and comet, is built in the system to accomplish the role and the responsibility of the individual purpose for the entire purpose, forms the harmony and the order and revolves them perfectly, based on the rule of the universe. There is no reason not to accomplish in such a tiny presence as the earth.

What kind of world would be built if people in the entire world release their own egoism in the lower dimension called the individual desire, build a world in which everybody can select their own life's work as the most favorite thing for the entire earth, and shoulder the Self-responsibility of Self-determination of the life that can form the perfect collaboration, and complete each role and responsibility?

When the individual entity accomplishes its own role and responsibility of the individual purpose for the entire purpose, it will be given and enjoy the equal value with the entire purpose evenly, based on the principle of the dimensional integration of the universe. Like a cell of the sole and a cell of the brain are directed to accomplish the role and the responsibility of the individual purpose for the entire body, when the consciousness is going to be directed from the individual to the family, the ethnic groups, the nation, and the world, each person is able to be given and enjoy the equal value, and it doesn't matter which part of the role and the responsibility you are in.

We should remove the border of each nation and share the role and the responsibility of the individual subjectively in each region, build the assembly organization and the nation with people who really like, for instance, agriculture, fishery, or industry, up to the national level as much as possible. It will become possible to direct to make global collaboration by placing the right person in the right place throughout the world in various types of occupations such as technical and medical, by selecting the most environmentally adapted assembly organization and the nation according to the role and the responsibility, and by making cultural exchange of strong individuality through the entire world freely at a desired time, and in a desired extent.

Even our 60 trillion cells are in perfect collaboration, so there is no reason that only 60 billion people cannot make the same kind of collaboration. The religions in the lower dimension should not exist in the center of the culture, like our past history, but it will become an important outstanding matter of concern to build the society, the nation, and the world where the individuality of each person exists in the center of the culture, hereafter.

We must establish the paradigm revolution globally in the 21st century, otherwise the entire earth will suffer from a calamity of religious struggle and it will be inevitable to go through a path of destruction by *nuclear*.

4-81. Individual subjectivity leads historical evolution

Based on the cosmological evidence, *we are always forced to exist by being directed to a higher spiritual dimension, by the relative universal original power based on the subjective love and freedom of SHINSEI, which is the verity of the individual entity of the universe.* Therefore, the spiritual consciousness entity, as our individual mental entity, creates the relative original power between SHINSEI and the "soul mind," the relative subjectivity, evokes the consciousness based on love, and directs to Self-Enlightenment and spiritual evolution by making Self-completion of the individual art to the creation of happiness based on the motivation of the individuality as the subject.

Based on this rule, the history of the evolution of the universe has become possible to sustain. As the individual subjectivity has become the guide for evolution, in the physical body it has formed face and figure through genes, individually, and in the spiritual consciousness entity it has formed as the complex individual substance of the personality and the spirituality up to the mind and the soul. Each of the individual subjectivities direct the way they want to go, and the process of evolutional history in the universe has been led by them, so there are no two things existing in the universe that are the same.

History has always been directed to evolution based on the principle of dimensional integration of love, opened the path of inner feelings to the higher spiritual dimension and completed as the individual art, by the impulsive exercise of the consciousness of love called the creation of happiness. The fact exists that the life entity has achieved evolution to the higher dimension, and still now it makes possible for sustainable evolution.

All individualities existing in the universe work to be integrated to the relative universal original power which is the integrated love consciousness in the universe, and SHINSEI works to find the objective art of happiness in the individuality of each person. In order to derive the relative original power to achieve rapid spiritual evolution, we should exercise the individual subjectivity to complete love in the higher spiritual dimension and the greater happiness of the worldly dimension, as the entire purpose.

4-82. Individuality integrates subject of love and object of happiness

We are going to walk through the process to release ONSHU connoted inside ourselves, in stages of the tangible substantial world which is the whole creator world to the human world, and the intangible substantial world which is the spiritual world.

The mission of human beings as the primate of all creation is to integrate the all creation world by love, so we must love all things in the creation world and relate to them with love from their point of view. Therefore, we should derive the relative original power of love with the universal original power which is contained in all existing things, open the path with inner feelings of happiness, and love all things involved as individual objects. By doing this, we can release ONSHU of the mineral dimension, the plant dimension, the animal dimension, and the human dimension, which is everything in the creation world.

Those who live the way of life of PARAREVO release their own ONSHU, by expanding the real freedom and the range of love, and aim to direct the creative happiness to the higher dimension. We should recognize that all objects involved in our life are an inevitable connection with us for releasing all ONSHU inside ourselves. Because when we become relative to all existing things as the object of the individual art of happiness, SHINSEI as the impulsive love in us and the spiritual consciousness entity create the energy by the relative original power, and exercise unconditionally. Then, SHINSEI of the universe, which is the relative universal original power of love of the universe, causes the synergistic resonance phenomenon with our inner SHINSEI and the greater creation of happiness will exercise inevitably as the individual art.

This means that SHINSEI is the common denominator, because we can connect with the spiritual world of the universe though SHINSEI. This is the system which induces the collaboration phenomenon and synergistic resonance of happiness setting up in the rule of the universe.

We are able to derive the relative original power of the higher dimension and make the individual art full growth by connecting the relative wave as the subject of love and all existing things as the object. As a result, when we go to the spiritual world of the universe after release from the body, we are able to revel in the creation of free love as the individual art in the intangible substantial world.

4- 83. The principle of integration of love and the principle of domination of ONSHU

To accomplish the transcendental Self-completion means to be released from the principle of dimensional integration of ONSHU on the earth star, and be directed to the principle of dimensional integration of love in the universe.

When examining the system and the mechanism of the earth star from the cosmological evidence of the higher dimension, the principle of dimensional integration of ONSHU on the earth is *the spiritual consciousness entity (the presence in the higher dimension) is dominated by the body (the presence in the lower dimension) and the body dominates and directs the spiritual consciousness entity to inconvenience.* The system of the human body is dominated by the organs, the organs are dominated by the tissue, the tissue is dominated by the cells, the cells are dominated by the genes, the genes are dominated by water, the water molecule is dominated by oxygen, and as a result, our body is dominated by oxygen. This is the physical domination structure of the respiratory function, which is fate for the body.

However, since the opposite things derive and disappear synchronically and simultaneously by the rule of entropy relativity, and are forced to exist by being directed to the relative subjectivity based on the rule of "spirit is subjective and body is objective," the principle of dimensional integration of love in the universe is: *the body is comprehended to the spiritual consciousness entity and the spiritual consciousness entity aims to make the body integrate and evolve by directing to the higher level.* As this rule is given priority, we have accomplished physical evolution as well as spiritual evolution. The role and the responsibility of the individual purpose are completed by directing to the entire purpose, from the genes to the cells, to the tissues and to the organs of our body, so that it becomes possible for us to exist as a human being, by the collaboration system which forms the harmony and the order toward the consciousness of the entire purpose.

Chapter Four ☆ The Conclusion

4-84. The earth star is the planet of legalized domination structure

The purpose of the domination structure in the depth psychology of human beings is making the priority concept for being inconvenient, so the consciousness of the domination structure is always completed by the corroboration of the consciousness and the deed based on the motivation.

According to the equation of dimensional domination, *the corroboration of the consciousness in which things in the lower dimension try to dominate things in the higher dimension, the consciousness exercises by the relative original power based on the rule of exclusion theory by jealousy by sorrow and ONSHU, and it causes our words and deeds based on the motivation of domination of the forcible displacement of a superior by the inferior by dividing and destroying the things in the higher dimension.* For instance, having complaints about superiors is commonplace, so the motivation which becomes the source of all kinds of evil is directed toward interruption, destruction, and domination, by *the rule of the exclusion theory by jealousy,* which are envy and jealousy.

Formerly, the proletariats were jealous of the bourgeoisies, and evoked the communist revolution, built a strong authoritarian dominating nation, and the nation leaders confiscated the freedom, property, and life of the people. However, since the ONSHU and the consciousness of destruction follow until the end, the communist nation was finally forced to go the path of Self-destruction, and was collapsed by the people by *the rule of the exclusion theory by jealousy.*

In other words, the system of the earth star began by the oxygen domination, reached to the genetic domination, expanded to the physical domination, the family domination, the social domination, the ethnic domination, and the national domination, and the dominating structure has been legalized openly throughout history, and functioned in all kinds of systems. Human beings have been tamed by the domination structure and inconvenience, without any feelings of contradiction.

4-85. The dominating structure of the brain is the center of physical domination

The spiritual consciousness entity has been tamed in the process of evolution in 3.8 billion years by the physical dominating structure which is the instinctive survival consciousnesses by the genetic domination.

The center of the physical domination is in the brain. So, what kind of structure does the brain have? The brain which has been in complete control of the central nerves through the brain cells by the genetic domination and controlling the hormonal and peripheral nerves, has succeeded in dominating the cells of the entire body. As a result, the brain succeeded in dominating the center of the instinctive survival consciousnesses by genetic domination, which means the brain is controlling the wisdom and the desire, and we human beings are reining at the top of the food chain.

The genetic information inherited to the genes of the brain cells has been preserved as memories in the genes of the brain cells as new information of the instinctive remaining consciousness of a higher dimension, by preservation by inscription. This instinct

Chapter Four ☆ The Conclusion

has controlled the desire without disappearing, and worked as the wisdom to accomplish the environmental adaptation in order to make the life of the body continue, and worked as the desire to dominate others, making human beings evolve up to this point. The center of the physical desire consciousness is controlled by overconcentration of the genes, which dominate the brain cells, and human beings have come to rein at the top of the life entities on the earth star.

The cells of the sole would never manifest the desire consciousness. The cells of the stomach have no claim on the appetite. The appetite center in the brain analyzes the information which came from the stomach, whether it is hunger or fullness, and controls the dietary desire. Other organs such as the liver and the pancreas have the consciousness as well but would never manifest the desire consciousness, and they are all controlled by the brain.

Since our five senses, seeing, taste, smell, touch, and hearing are also all managed by the brain, and the brain analyzes them and catches as the senses, all memories and senses will be destroyed at the moment the brain is destroyed. For the supporting phenomenon of this, people who are brain-dead never demonstrate their desires, and even the memories of the past are destroyed and not preserved. Therefore, it is proof that we are enslaved by the desire domination of the brain, and have the common ecological behaviors by the common desire consciousness from bacteria to human beings. It doesn't matter if we build status, reputation and property, we will lose everything together with memories, which we created in this world, at the moment the brain is destroyed, even though we are still alive.

There is a well-known story told by the wife of a professor emeritus of a prestigious university. She said when the professor got Alzheimer's, shortly after his retirement, he was playing with his own excrement, putting it on his body and clothes, in his study. Since he only studied his specialty in his university but nothing else, which called "an expert ignoramus," the reality is that he has not achieved the spiritual evolution as the condition of the spiritual consciousness entity, by the functional disorder of the brain. It is caused by the fact that he was intoxicated by the brain domination, obtained the honor as he wished, and only became arrogant by being drowned in the title as a professor emeritus at the famous university, however his soul has not grown beyond the level of a baby. Because of the destruction of the brain, it was converted from the rule of "body is subjective and spirit is objective" to the rule of "spirit is subjective and body is objective," and the condition of the soul based on the spiritual dimension was manifested realistically.

The spiritual world has nothing to do with the quality of brain, but it is the determination how the person completed the personality formation and the spirituality formation to a higher spiritual dimension by releasing the physical world benefits. We should live in the Now by making Self-completion with the great virtue of unselfishness by Self-sacrifice, according to the rule of "the attainment of the spiritual being during life" by the way of life of PARAREVO.

Chapter Four ☆ The Conclusion

4-86. The physical dominating structure is the root of all evil in the rule of reincarnation

The excessive physical world benefits, material pleasure, and worldly desires for acquisition of the relative evaluation, are all exercised and manifested by the genetic domination, which controls the brain cells. In Buddhism, it is said that *108 worldly desires* exist in the brain.

When the soul, the spiritual consciousness entity, gets free from the physical domination, it is cut off at the pineal gland in the brain stem, which is the center of the aggregation of the worldly desires, released from the seventh (Sahasrara) chakra, archives disembodiment and goes to the spiritual world, the intangible substantial world. The time of completion of disembodiment will become very important.

The soul which spent life in this world by the value for the acquirement of excessive physical benefits and relative evaluation, has a strong attachment to this world by physical domination, and it will take a long time from the moment the heart stops and the last breath is released from the oxygen domination.

As I mentioned before, the tangible earth where we are living, is covered by the atmosphere. This is called the physical barrier. Also, there is a spiritual barrier, "the River" for the intangible earth. Because of this spiritual barrier, our souls are not able to go to the intangible earth freely from the tangible earth. This time period, which is *eight hours* in the earth time, is the time limit as to whether or not the soul is released from physical domination and can pass to the intangible substantial world. If it takes more than eight hours, the soul cannot cross "the River." Most souls cross "the River" and go to the spiritual world of the earth, which is the intangible substantial world. If a person had an unusual life such as drug dependence or criminal activity, or committed suicide, it will take more than eight hours to cross "the River" and could possibly become "ghost bound" to a specific physical location, and remain in the earth plane.

Even though the soul went to the intangible earth world within the eight hours, it still carries the habit of the worldly attachment with Self-trapped physical dominating consciousness in the tangible world, so the soul continues to live in inconvenience. The spiritual consciousness entity which has not trained to transcend the theoretical framework and value of the earth star, will repeat this world again and again according to the rule of reincarnation. The existing religious doctrines are for the repeater school of the earth star, the prison planet, so they continue to be dominated by the rule of reincarnation, eternally.

When we become the cosmic life entity, since the cosmic life basis is the zero time period, we secede from the body and cross the earth barrier immediately after death, and we would not go to the spiritual world of the earth (the intangible earth), but go to the cosmic world (the spiritual world of the universe) and never return to the earth.

4-87. The dominating structure on the earth star is unique structure of the universe

We should always aim for the way of life of PARAREVO, which integrates the spiritual consciousness as the subject and the physical consciousness as the object, in order to accomplish spiritual evolution to a higher spiritual dimension. However, since the fated role and responsibility on the earth star are directed to physical domination, the fact is that we are not able to live in this world by ignoring the physical consciousness.

For the life entities on the earth star shouldering the contradicted double structure as the fate, I am compelled to understand that probably, on the basis of *the existing purpose of the earth star,* there is the role and responsibility to make the spiritual consciousness entity subordinate and direct it to inconvenience by restraining the physical theoretical framework and the value centered in the body.

The life entity in such a mechanism and system is extremely rare in the universe. Most of the life entities in the universe are basically the spiritual consciousness entity level or higher, but there are a few life entities shouldering the body. Otherwise, we would not need such a huge, infinite universe.

4-88. Manifestation of SHINSEI integration consciousness world by PARAREVO

Since the spiritual consciousness entity is captured and restricted by the physical body, in order for us to accomplish transcendental Self-completion, *we must integrate our emotions by becoming SHINSEI unity which is the similar presence of the verity of the individual entity which is the subject of love called SHINSEI, and the individual mental entity which is the object of happiness called "I," by the fundamental relative universal original power.* We should open the path of inner feelings by creating the relative original power of SHINSEI unity, release the physical domination by transcending the physical senses by manifesting the individual art of sensitivity and feelings based on free love, and achieve Self-completion in this world.

It will be possible to establish the internal world (the spiritual consciousness entity) which is the spiritual quality world in the higher spiritual dimension, by opening the path toward the feeling of happiness for all things involved, with SHINSEI as the common denominator, according to the sensitivity based on love and causing the synergistic resonance phenomenon. And doing so, we also integrate the external world (body and materials) with love and manifest the individual art of a higher internal world. This preparation is inevitable for us to go to the intangible substantial world.

When we establish the perfect collaboration which completes co-existence, mutual prosperity and symbiosis, by the way of life of PARAREVO in this world, we can create a guidepost for regeneration of SHINSEI and the soul, which has evolved to the life entity of a new spiritual dimension, integrate to love of the universal dimension by transcending the category of the earth dimension. It will be possible to manifest the true way of life of PARAREVO, for the first time, if we can transcend all values of the earth dimension, and reform them to the category and the paradigm of the universal dimension.

So, we must practice the way of life of PARAREVO, and free the spiritual consciousness entity by releasing physical domination, transcend excessive physical world benefits and the relative evaluation, and train to manifest the SHINSEI integration consciousness world wherein we can enjoy the individual art freely. Achieving transcendental Self-completion means to experience and feel the SHINSEI integration consciousness world beyond the body and the verge of life and death while we are in this world, and release physical domination and make the spiritual consciousness entity free, embody the practice of love and the creation of happiness, and manifest the individual art freely.

4-89. The true view of life and death based on the rule of "the attainment of the spiritual being during life"

We need to quickly improve the negative legacy built up through the 20th century such as rapid environmental destruction in the natural world by the science civilization and mass consumption of energies, and moral hazard in the social order. The largest negative legacy in the 20th century was the advent of nuclear weapons such as the atomic bomb. It was like opening Pandora's box. So, it is not too much to say that life entities on the earth are in the hands of human beings. It is impossible to avoid this crisis with the existing theoretical framework and value built through the 20th century by religions and thought, and we now have intense stress and frustration building up all over the world, so we are on the brink of a crisis of an explosive situation.

The essence of paradigm of the way of life of PARAREVO is *all things existing in the entire universe, including SHINSEI and the universe itself, are forced to exist synchronically and simultaneously, by the relative original power with the slight fluctuation of imperfection between the relative universal original power based on freedom and love of SHINSEI, and the universal original power contained the nature of SHINSEI.*

Therefore, there is no unique and absolute existence called God in the universe. The entire universe is a relative and interactive integrated world called *SHINSEI integration consciousness entity.* Based on this rule of the universe, in the 21st century, it is urgent to establish the true purpose of life and view of life and death by the way of life of PARAREVO with each person, rather than occupying the view of life and the view of death with the theoretical framework and value through the 20th century. By this rule, it will be possible to solve all problems.

The theory of life based on the cosmological evidence is based on the rule of entropy relativity, and it exists instantly by being completed, by *the rule of "the attainment of the spiritual being during life"* in which life and death derive synchronically and simultaneously. The absolute difference between the life entity in the universe and the life entity on the earth is this. The life entity in the universe completes the spherical structure by the pair system of SHINSEI and SHINSEI integration structure and then creates the sustainable energy eternally based on the rule of dimensional integration, and it will become possible to exist eternally as the spiritual life entity, digitally, by transcending the time axis. The life entity on the earth forms the three layer compound structure by the triangle system of the physical dominating structure of SHINSEI, the spiritual consciousness entity, and the body, based on the rule of dimensional domination, and exists in analog.

Because of this ignorance toward the true view of life and death on the earth, as the nature of the prison star, the life entity on the earth has attached to the physical life in this world, and continued to seek immortality since the beginning of history. Moreover, the attachment toward this physical life and the anxiety and fear toward death become the source of the various negative legacies built in human history.

In the 21st century, we should be released from all anxiety, fear, and attachment by building the view of life and the view of death based on rule of "the attainment of the spiritual being during life" transcend the fear of the fate that the body will be destroyed eventually. There is no anxiety and fear at all in the theoretical framework and value of the way of life of PARAREVO, which transcend the life and death of the body. In the PARAREVO way, the excessive physical world benefits and the attachment for it will be completely meaningless and insignificant, and the pyramidal dominating structure based on the evil competition principle will collapse and become nothing, and it will be possible to build the collaboration world by the spherical integrated structure. In the near future, the existing religious theories and the earth logical values will be destroyed worldwide by the PARAREVO theory.

4-90. The 21st century is the watershed in human history

I believe that the culture and civilization that human beings have built up through the 20th century has reached a great turning point. One way we human beings can go is either to continue to destroy the natural environment by strengthening the paradigm up through the 20th century, promoting the science almighty doctrine, and taking priority in the economic supreme doctrine, and invite the end on a global scale by the civil reason, or invite the end on a global scale by the cultural reason with weapons of mass destruction, by the struggle of the theoretical framework and value of monotheism in Europe and Middle Eastern Asia. Or we can choose the other way which is to rebuild new theoretical framework and value on a global scale by releasing the civilization and the culture we had built up through the 20th century, and complete the collaboration world globally beyond race, ethnic group, and nation.

It is clear that the time will soon come when we need a great change on the global scale. Regarding the global warming issue, the situation is that we are not able to obtain the consensus easily, due to the expectations of interests among the developed countries, and continue bargaining. Also, light and shadow of the economic supremacy doctrine in the developed countries has spread, and the economic disparity appears remarkably in the northern and southern hemispheres with the equator as a dividing line. Also in the EU nations, the economic disparity spreads between the northern and the southern areas, based on the rule of entropy relativity. Rich countries in the developed nations become richer, but on the other hand, the poor countries in the undeveloped nations are suffering in poverty and hunger.

Considering the population issue, the developed nations are in agony due to a trend towards having fewer children, and the undeveloped nations are suffering from a population explosion. In order to resolve problems, one by one, which are piling up all over the world, we must spread the theoretical framework and the value of the way of life of PARAREVO to the world, and reform all kinds of theoretical frameworks and values radically and integrate them to one by directing the one world family doctrine.

4-91. How do we resolve discrimination in the world?

In the mechanized universal system, which was created by the rule of entropy relativity based on the cosmological evidence, opposite things must exist, synchronically and simultaneously. For instance, there is a rich country as well as a poor country, and there is a peaceful country as well as a warring country.

If we try to solve this problem, there are two methods. One is to convert the paradigm to make the one-nation world doctrine, and all nations in the entire earth equally become one rich and peaceful country. However, there are many difficulties we have to overcome, such as the wall between wealth and poverty, the wall of race, ethnic groups, nation, civilization, culture (religions), and languages, etc. When we try to transcend such difficult obstacles, we have to face great burdens and risks, so it is difficult to resolve problems by the current paradigm.

Another method is to just keep all the walls, but change the consciousness of each person to the way of life of PARAREVO and evolve the spiritual nature itself. With this method we do not need to take extra risks, but are able to reform easily without any burden. Since all the walls built around us are related to the personality history and are based on Self-determination, we should convert to the way of life to achieve Self-completion with Self-responsibility by the way of life of PARAREVO, which is the acceptance for everything, unconditionally and totally. So, the external conversion comes with a big risk and will invite conflict and struggle. On the other hand, since the internal conversion is to direct the real existing purpose and the existing value as human beings it should not carry any risks. However, the wall is still standing in the way of finding the real purpose and values, and this wall is caused by the religious problems.

Thus, since we have charged into the religious struggle era in the 21st century, we may invite unexpected results on a global scale if the world neglects and does not control this problem. It is no exaggeration to say that the future of the earth depends on how human beings draw a mental design as the future prospect and make the concrete ground design on a global scale. In order to do this, we need to change all paradigms in the earth dimension level to the theoretical framework and value in the universal dimension; otherwise, it would be impossible.

Changing the theories and logics of the earth to the rules and principles of the universe means to distinguish the difference between knowledge and consciousness and change the concept of life and policy, oppositely. Knowledge is to understand presumption and supposition made by the brain. The presumption and supposition made by human beings are, for example, time, science, economics, property, reputation, theory of good and evil, God, etc., and most people go from kindergarten through university to learn those theories. On the other hand, consciousness is to understand and accept the dimension of the facts, which the spiritual consciousness entity experienced as truth. Since we cannot distinguish between knowledge and consciousness, we are easily tamed by an envelope of lies by the brain domination. We must connect with others as the spiritual consciousness entity with truth rather than with the envelope of lies, while we are in this world.

4-92. How do we resolve the gap between rich and poor?

The rich nation understands the situation of the poor nation by information only, but those who live in a poor country do not have any information, so they have no choice but to face reality and live every day by doing their best. So, what should we do in order to solve this disparity of wealth and poverty, cosmologically? Since the rule of the universe follows the principle of dimensional integration based on the rule of "spirit is subjective and body is objective," there is no energy required when the higher potential goes down to the lower potential, it goes automatically and works unconditionally to form the harmony and order equally, according to the rule of balance.

However, the system of the earth has a totally opposite vector, so rich people become richer and richer, and poor people become poorer and poorer, which increases the disparity of wealth and poverty, economically. It is because the rule of the earth follows the principle of dimensional integration based on the rule of "body is subjective and spirit is objective," so, greedy people who have the motivation for exploitation for the excessive physical world benefits, which are evoked from human desire egoism, have reigned at the top of the terrestrial world.

The subject of responsibility for this world is in the rich nations of the developed countries, not in the poor nations of the undeveloped countries. According to the equation of spiritual evolution, when we accept the poor and severe environment by love, it will be possible for us to make spiritual evolution to a higher spiritual dimension, and it means that the opposite truth of the earth logical evidence is proven cosmologically. It is said that "it is more difficult for a rich man to enter heaven than it is for a camel to go through the eye of a needle" or "Blessed are the poor: for theirs is the kingdom of heaven." So, if those words are not true, the universe would be unequal. If the richness of material does not make the poorness of mind, and the poorness of material does not make the richness of mind, the meaning and the significance for the conception descent for spiritual evolution would be lost.

Since the PARAREVO theory is a paradoxical theory, those who are directed to the benefits for the spiritual world can understand more and easily make spiritual evolution, than those who are blessed by the fortunes of physical world benefits.

Therefore, when the advanced nations understand the existing purpose and the existing value of this world beyond the verge of life and death, by establishing the real view of life and death, based on the rule of the "attainment of the spiritual being during life," all things of the rich countries will be restored to the poor countries automatically without any burden, by the concept of the way of life of PARAREVO.

4-93. How do we resolve the disparity in civilization?

The scientific civilization has been made by the correspondence of the era based on the spiritual evolution. Since the culture and

Chapter Four ☆ The Conclusion

the civilization have sailed together on the winds of time, neither of them has developed disorderly and unilaterally. The culture I am talking about here is not the religious theoretical framework and value which is the existing incompetent relic of the past, but originates from the evolution of personality and spirituality based on the standard for the "soul mind" of human nature which has achieved spiritual evolution in each era according to the principle of dimensional integration.

We can say that the underdeveloped countries are spiritually underdeveloped, however, from now on, a reversal phenomenon will occur between the developed countries and the underdeveloped countries according to the rule of relative change based on entropy relativity. The education and the popularization of the PARAREVO theory are necessary for the underdeveloped countries. There are many adults and children who are not even able to read or write in those countries, so when they are given language education and learn the way of life of PARAREVO, we will see an amazing difference. They will achieve spiritual evolution rapidly, and easily leave the advanced countries behind. This is the reason for the Bible saying that "And indeed there are last who will be first, and there are first who will be last" (Luke 13:30, NKJV).

Why is that? Because of the arrogance and the conceit of the advance countries, they are occupied with the theoretical framework and value of the physical world benefits, and their Self-defense and store of vested interests make it very difficult to accept the theoretical framework and the value of the way of life of PARAREVO. On the other hand, in the undeveloped countries, their sentimental world and personality dimension are equal to a blank canvas. Since there is no theoretical framework and value hold on the excessive physical world benefits, they do not have anything to lose and have limitless opportunities, so it is easy for them to understand and accept the PARAREVO theory.

In the 21st century, a new civilization era will come to the developing countries and will manifest the social structure of collaboration by the PARAREVO theory, and lead the world. We should give the PARAREVO education to the "universe's favored" undeveloped countries and let it spread.

4-94. How do we resolve the religious conflicts?

Religion is the fundamental power to build civilizations. It is not too much to say that there are as many civilizations existing in the world as there are religions. So, one's identity could be determined by the religious theoretical frameworks and values. Today, religious terrorism has become a global threat, which derives from the difference in the theoretical frameworks and the values of the religious doctrines, and they are repeating wars like the Crusades. Unless new theoretical frameworks and values appear and integrate all religions to one, which will surpass and transcend the existing religious theoretical frameworks and values, it will be impossible to avoid this threat.

Instead of petroleum energy, there are new alternative energies coming popular and the world economic picture over the role of oil money centered in the Middle East is changing. They will be able to choose to become inhabitants of the desert again by losing the riches they obtained once, or they may release the weapons of

Chapter Four ☆ The Conclusion

mass destruction that were the accumulated negative legacy to the world. When an extremely delicate crisis situation is brought on by fanatical fundamentalists of monotheism who are losing oil money, a global threat will come inevitably as reality, by opening Pandora's box to nuclear bombs.

And, the existence of China where in the government official society that has a unique background of Confucianism philosophy and Socialism, which is extremely poisoned by materialistic egotism, are compounded and have formed peculiar morality, so when China plays a central role in the global economy, it will become a great threat in the world. The children in China who have been raised by dependence constitution with vital domination desire under the overprotection of fondness according to the one-child policy, which is the worst mistake in human history, become the central presence in the country by winning the evil competition principle, the moral hazard of China will be expanded in a heartbeat, and the global competition for economic supremacy will become more serious, and the threat and disorder in the world will flow over.

The issues on the earth will be completed by the role and the responsibility of the people on the earth. It is because the rule of the universe is *led by Self-determination, Self-responsibility, and Self-completion under the rule of freedom. Therefore, it is equal.* The universe and even Gods carry through *the principle of nonaggression and nonintervention* toward the earth. In order to guarantee the rule of freedom, the principle of Self-responsibility must be secured.

There is only one way to avoid religious strife. We must propagate the PARAREVO theory globally as soon as possible, integrate the religions under the cosmological evidence, change the theoretical frameworks and values of monotheism, return to SHINSEI, which is the common denominator of the life entities in the entire universe, connoted in each person, and complete SHINSEI integration consciousness of SHINSEI unity of each person.

4-95. Free from the boundaries between race and nations

The problem of those boundaries is extremely serious, and even religions have not been able to solve them. Why is that? It is because there are influences of invisible power far beyond the religious values. There are the presences of historical indigenous Gods called guardian deities of one's birthplace in the background of races and nations. They are the strong existing energy which spiritually integrates each region. They are far transcending the religious theoretical frameworks and values, which is the reason why conflicts, such as among Christianity and Islam, happen everywhere and never cease.

When we see this fact, we realize that religions are not helpful at all, and are not even able to manage the conflicts. So, we have to have strong doubts about the presence of religions. We must question whether religions are just for religions or for humans and the world, because it is not possible to build the collaboration world the way the existing religions bring about terrorism, conflicts and wars.

The exercise of the human consciousness and the words and deeds based on motivation are done according to the rule of the

Chapter Four ☆ The Conclusion

relative original power based on mind and spirit. There exists the internal relative original power and the external relative original power in the relative original power based on mind and spirit. When we understand this rule completely, we can basically solve all problems.

The internal relative original power is the creation original power of mind and spirit which is created or derived by the relative original power between one's own mind, which is based on the personality formation history in this life, and the soul, which is based on the spirituality formation history through the past life. Therefore, the exercise of the consciousness will change greatly by learning the PARAREVO theory and practicing the way of life of PARAREVO.

The problem is the external relative original power. The formation process of mind is the same as the internal relative original power; however, the spirituality entity involving our mind is totally different, since it comes from outside. Our exercising consciousness will be totally different depending on what kind of spirituality entity we would be involved with. For example, whether we are linked with the spirituality entity in the higher dimension or the spirituality entity in the poor and lower spiritual dimension filled with ugliness, the relative original power based on mind and spirit will be significantly different.

In the physical life, we have a person in charge in our area, such as mayor of the city, or governor, or prime minister, based on the rule of "body is subjective and soul is objective," and in the spiritual world there are guardian deities of each birthplace. Those deities are the indigenous Gods which have existed relatively in each place and ruled the region spiritually throughout history, based on the rule of "spirit is subjective and body is objective." Since the guardian deity of each birthplace and the soul are extremely human like, so they can carry envy, jealousy, anger or even be ill-natured. When they are in a good mood, they respond to the requests of the human world quite easily. They also have extremely human like preferences, which can greatly differ depending on the culture and customs of each region.

I am not talking about the physical world benefits we would like to gain by praying to the gods, but about how we complete in this world by releasing the historical ONSHU of races and peoples. The indispensable thing for this is to release the spiritual ONSHU relating to the races and nations, and this becomes a great driving force to change history. This method is completed by the substantial work and the spiritual work. If the head of a nation who is responsible for people's lives, clears up the past, which is the historical spiritual ONSHU, and completes the spiritual work and the substantial work toward the nation which holds the historical ONSHU, *to release the ONSHU of its own nation by loving the ONSHU,* the spiritual ONSHU will be released by the rule of preservation by inscription.

This is the same as the relationship between victim and offender. On the earth, we consider it is natural for the offender to apologize, however, in this way, we only preserve ONSHU over the ONSHU and repeat the antagonized-relationship forever, and do not reach any solution. People who live the way of life of PARAREVO know that the equation to release ONSHU is based on the equation of spiritual evolution which is to *"release one's own ONSHU by loving the ONSHU."* The responsibility of offender and victim are directed in paradox, but people living the PARAREVO way understand how the victim side should face toward the offender side, with what kind of sentimental world and personality dimension.

As an example, it makes a huge difference in the fortune of the nation, whether we Japanese keep our ONSHU toward the Unites States for dropping the atomic bomb, or not.

According to the rule of exclusion theory by jealousy, the victim would be directed to Self-destruction and Self-collapse by blaming, criticizing, expelling and excluding the offender with hatred and hard feelings, but on the other hand, he/she would be directed toward creation and prosperity by loving, forgiving and tolerating the offender. According to this equation, if the heads of the nations in the world settle the past ONSHU of the nation by the substantial work, then at the same time the spiritual work will be completed to release the spiritual ONSHU which has been preserved throughout history, based on the rule of preservation by inscription.

4-96. Equation for releasing core of ONSHU

The core of ONSHU in the terrestrial life is in us. We have been building the ONSHU of the spiritual consciousness entity, continuously, by the two major desire consciousnesses of the body which are the instinctive survival consciousnesses. This is because we human beings are the three layer structure of the triangle system of SHINSEI, the spiritual consciousness entity, and the body, so this makes the triangle relationship of SHINSEI, the "soul mind," and the "body mind." In this triangle system, "soul mind" and "body mind" compete for SHINSEI, and have brought up various problems and made them complicated.

Human beings have been tamed by those instinctive survival consciousnesses throughout 3.8 billion years, strengthened endless desires and reined at the top of the food chain in the terrestrial life. We have now become the most greedy and dangerous creatures among the terrestrial lives. We are the result of continuing to increase the quality and the quantity of the desires by strengthening the physical dominating structure without any change while we are maintaining the rule of "body is subjective and soul is objective." We are invaded by the dependence of physical desire, by seeking the pleasures of physical world benefits, like falling into drug addiction. "We know it is not good but we cannot stop doing it." In the universe, we human beings are rare and foolish life entities with inconvenience.

The life entity in the higher spiritual dimension in the universe has the function to create sustainable relative original power in the slight fluctuation of imperfection by the pair system of SHINSEI and the spiritual consciousness entity, and it directs the creation and the development to a higher level and provides the system which is possible to exist eternally, by the mechanism of the spherical integration. Unless we change our system from the three layer structure of the triangle system, SHINSEI, the spiritual consciousness entity, and the body, to the two layer structure, the pair system of SHINSEI and the spiritual consciousness entity, and achieve spiritual evolution to SHINSEI integrated life entity, it is impossible to become a free life entity existing in the infinite universe. We must get rid of the mechanism of the earth star; otherwise we human beings will continue to repeat the inconvenient

Chapter Four ☆ The Conclusion

earth life forever.

In order for human beings to achieve spiritual evolution to a new cosmic life entity, we should complete our assignment and responsibility on the earth star. Since the earth star is the prison planet from the universal dimension, we are all offenders but not victims. Therefore, as long as we fall into victim consciousness by being occupied with the theory of good and evil on the earth dimension and direct to shifting responsibility, the responsibility of our assignment would not be completed, and we will continue re-descending according to the rule of reincarnation, eternally.

The responsibility of our assignment is connoted in each of us and exists as the core of ONSHU. Based on the rule of entropy relativity, the spiritual consciousness entity directs to form the core of love according to the rule of "spirit is subjective and body is objective" and the physical body directs to form the core of ONSHU according to the rule of "body is subjective and spirit is objective."

The real ONSHU *exists not in the distance but near us,* so the closest ONSHU for the individual soul is the existence of the body. Beyond the individual level, the second closest ONSHU for us is the relationship between parent and child, and the third one is between siblings, and the fourth is the one between a married couple. The vertical relationship of the parent-child is the most important one to form the core of love and ONSHU of the spiritual consciousness entity. It determines, unconsciously, whether it directs to Self-Enlightenment and spiritual evolution according to the principle of dimensional integration of love, or directs to the poor Self-Enlightenment and spiritual degeneration according to the principle of dimensional domination of ONSHU.

Even though the spiritual consciousness entity had the Self-determination of genes and parents, under free intention, and to descend by conception in order to accomplish spiritual evolution, according to the rule of reincarnation based on the rule of "spirit is subjective and body is objective," if the soul descended to poor genes and parents, far from the expectation or contrary to the expectation prospect, the disillusionment toward Self-determination would be specifically toward Self-hatred and Self-denial, automatically and unconsciously, and restored to one's own self as ONSHU by the rule of adaptation.

The most ugly and poor things for human beings are Self-hatred and Self-denial. They are the biggest core of ONSHU and the root of evil. The relationship between parent and child shoulders the biggest assignment in the personality formation history, and has the greatest influence on Self-Enlightenment and spiritual evolution, and it also becomes the blind spot of love of the Mobius' loop which easily Self-forms the core of love and ONSHU.

The Mobius loop of love is the mechanism to create eternal and sustainable energy as SHINSEI integration consciousness entity. It is the universal system to make sustainable creation and development, direct to the spiritual dimension of the higher level according to the principle of dimensional integration, by the mechanism of the relative original power which derives by the slight fluctuation of imperfection by the pair system between SHINSEI and the spiritual consciousness entity. This mechanism and the system, which when the "body mind" evokes at the same time the "soul mind" achieves the growth, will become sustainable by the rule of relative change of SHINSEI and the spiritual consciousness entity. When SHINSEI evokes evil by the relativity with the "body mind," it evokes good by the relativity between SHINSEI and the "soul mind," which is to surpass evil by good. This is called *the rule of relative change based on SHINSEI*.

Generally speaking, on the earth it is said that "forgiven because they are the parent-child," "forgiven because they are siblings," or "forgiven because they are a married couple," so that they conduct verbal abuse, violence, excessive interference and words and deeds between themselves which they would never use to others. However, in the PARAREVO world, the most fundamental concept is "not forgiven because they are the parent-child," "not forgiven because they are siblings" or "not forgiven because they are a married couple." Since they understand that their relationships are very valuable and connoting an important equation of the spiritual evolution, they make the Self-effort to build the relationship to respect the dignity of each other, to build the relationship to express all thoughts and mind, understand each other and care for each other, and create the core of love firmly by releasing the ONSHU.

Therefore, those who live the way of life of PARAREVO will never conduct the Self-escape to the world of Self-satisfaction and Self-intoxication, by being occupied with prayer to release the ONSHU. They persist in the undeniable existentialism, and achieve the Self-completion of Self-responsibility based on the equation of spiritual evolution, which is to love a person near you as *to release its own ONSHU by loving the ONSHU*.

4-97. Transition to female supremacy from male supremacy

The important thing in converting history and the only method to avoid the future crises of the earth is to convert all existing mechanisms and systems from the male type dominating structure to the female type integrating structure by spiritually wise women, as soon as possible.

The rule of the universal revolution is to direct to the intention of women, which are the relative subject, according to the principle of dimensional integration based on "spirit is subjective and body is objective." The intention of men, which are the relative object, should be comprehended to the intention of women, and the intention of women should direct the intention of men to the higher level and integrate all intentions.

So, the more spiritually wise women appear and manifest to the world, the more the society, the nations, and the world will regenerate, develop, and purify. This is the only path to real world peace. I must emphasize that in the younger generations, those who are not married yet, are responsible for the future and should learn and understand the PARAREVO theory. In order to do so, men should transfer all authority, power, and all kinds of male supremacy from their hands to women's hands, as soon as possible. For example, of the number of legislatures, government officials, and company executives, women should account for three quarters of them. It sounds like a very difficult change; however, unless *the supremacy devolution is completed under the responsibility of human beings, the earth star will remain as the prison planet forever.*

Since the spiritual evolution will be completed by being directed to the principle of dimensional integration, it is impossible to complete by the theory with men being the relative object, just like it is impossible for men to become pregnant and produce a new life to this world. By the conflicts with the religious theories based on *the logics of power, domination, struggles and destruction* by men, like Jesus and Buddha, as the relative object, history has already proven that it is absolutely impossible to complete spiritual evolution and graduate from the earth star.

This is because the equation of spiritual evolution is led to the relative subjectivity, women. According to the principle of dimensional integration based on *the logics of love, integration, harmony, and creation* of women, the physical quality improvement of the genetic recombination and the spiritual quality improvement of the principle of dimensional integration of motherly love, based on the rule of change by birth and re-birth in the womb which is the sanctuary of the spiritual evolution, and then, the physical evolution and the spiritual evolution are completed synchronically and simultaneously.

This has led the evolution process in history. Even though superficially it has been a male dominated world, the physical evolution and the spiritual evolution have been established in history in the womb for certain. As long as women bear the role and the responsibility for the change by birth and re-birth that direct to the most important life evolution, all authorities, roles, missions and responsibilities are given to women by the universe, for the change by birth and re-birth of society, nations, and the world.

Now we have been given the Cosmic Bible, which is the PARAREVO theory. This shows that if men who close the path which women should take, appear in the future, the path for them to live in the universe will be closed. This is because *the rights of approval in this world are held in the hands of men, however, the rights of approval in the spiritual world are all held by women.*

4-98. The way for solving problems on the earth

Where can we find the cause of evil on the earth star? It exists in the genes of each person. Two major desires in instinctive survival consciousnesses, which are the dietary desire and the sexual desire, have shifted according to the rule of the physical causality. The dietary desire has changed to the material desire, and the sexual desire has changed to the domination desire, the status desire and the reputation desire. Those desires are inherited as the instinctive remaining consciousnesses by genetic domination according to the rule of the genetic chain, and continuously succeeded to the physical dominating structure.

This mechanism, the rule of "body is subjective and spirit is objective," has firmly created a wall of ONSHU between races, nations, languages and cultures. Without shifting this desire consciousness, we are not able to solve all problems. Also, with the old-fashioned theoretical frameworks and values throughout history, human beings are eventually heading to the result of Self-destruction.

We only have one way to go if we want to resolve this problem. We should shift the world to the one family doctrine and direct

Chapter Four ☆ The Conclusion

to the global principle, integrated to one theory and rule. The method to integrate the world to one is not *inbreeding,* which makes undifferentiated sexual desire consciousness duplicated and produced people such as Adolf Hitler, but it transcends all cultures, civilizations and languages beyond races and nations, and expands in *"global mating"* with people who have no connection in DNA.

If we make "global mating" for the next seven generations, the physical quality improvement by genetic recombination will be done easily and it will reduce the instinctive remaining consciousnesses by half, and the desire consciousness of the body will be changed greatly, according to the rule of change by birth and re-birth based on the PARAREVO theory. As a result, there will be no wall of race or nation, and naturally, the struggles of the cultures, the disparities of the civilizations, and the gap of wealth and poverty, will be corrected. And, by the integration of each language in the world to one common language, I am sure that the global collaboration world will be established by the posterity of PARAREVO.

To do this, how fast we can produce many "spiritually wise women" all over the world, who can live the way of life of PARAREVO, is the most important outstanding problem. It is because the soul of the higher dimension of the new era *is descended by conception, by the rule of relative original power based on the mind and spirit according to the spiritual dimension of women.* Women should make the best Self-effort to conceive the sacred spirit by "the sacred conception relationship" in order to receive the soul of a higher spiritual dimension, but not conceive by conducting disgraceful and perverted "sexual relationships of the lower dimension" by the physical and sexual desire, according to the undifferentiated sexual desire consciousness. By doing so, it will be possible for women to open the path to their own spiritual dimension, and it will also become possible for both mother and child to complete Self-Enlightenment and spiritual evolution to a new stage.

Unless we hasten to proceed with the settlement for the problem of the undifferentiated sexual desire world as soon as possible, moral hazard will be spread, and the infection explosion of AIDS will occur, so we will be exposed to the threat of new microorganisms, and will reach the crisis for the collapse of human beings by the disgrace of sexuality and vicious crimes by undifferentiated sexual impulse.

The driving force for evolution is to be free from the sexual desire consciousness. On the other hand, by being dominated by this consciousness, the principle of dimensional domination functions and spiritual degeneration occurs. Lower organisms such as microorganisms, create new organisms by gene recombination and make a new threat. For example, according to the PARAREVO theory, the AIDS virus did not exist in human beings or in monkeys in the beginning. This is the result that a native African had conducted bestiality with a rhesus monkey. A human being of the higher dimension had a sexual desire toward a monkey in the lower dimension, and fell into sexual disgrace, so a virus in a lower organism was genetically modified and caused the new virus by the totally opposite process from the evolution according to the principle of dimensional domination.

Now, by the overflowing chaotic indecent sexual information and sexual disgrace worldwide, younger generations are becoming like Sodom and Gomorrah (it is said that the city of Sodom and Gomorrah in the Old Testament had fallen to depravity of sexual disgrace). If we continue to go as is, the explosion of infection by AIDS would inevitably occur, and moreover, we may face the crises of human collapse by microorganisms by making new viruses. Therefore, we urgently need to educate women in the world by the PARAREVO theory, promote global mating by international marriage, convert the flow of the rule of physical causality, and release all physical desire consciousnesses.

4-99. Challenge "the era of termination" in religions

We are living in the era in which 6,000 years has passed in the three stages of the first 2,000 years from Adam and Eve to Abraham and Sarah, the second 2,000 years to Jesus and Mary Magdalene, and the third 2,000 years to the present, and as the sacred revelation suggests against the termination ideology, now is the time that we are asked if we can accomplish true spiritual evolution in these modern times.

In 1991, the Soviet socialism, which was the symbol of communism, collapsed, so that the Cold War era was over as well as the end of the ideological struggle era, and we have entered into the religious struggle era. In the first year of the 21st century, on September 11, 2001, terrorist attacks were carried out against the USA by extremists of Islamic Fundamentalism, beginning with the twin towers of the World Trade Center. The collapse of two buildings, which were the symbol of American capitalism, suggests that it was indeed the end of the capitalist economy, and the ideological conflict axis between communism and capitalism, and it was converted into the era of religious struggle.

In the Buddhist Eschatology, it is said that 5,670,000,000 years after Buddha's death, Miroku (a Buddhist saint) finished training in Tusita Heaven, and after becoming Nyorai (a tathagata), descended to save all creatures and all life. However, this is not an astounding or absurd prophecy. The PARAREVO theory suggests that this number is not talking about 5,670,000,000 years, but *is the time when the human as the most greedy and dangerous creature on the earth, reigning at the top of the food chain, grows to 5,670,000,000 population, after the death of Buddha.*

It was said that the global population in the era of the Old Testament of Adam and Eve, 6,000 years ago, was only 6,000,000. And in the era of Buddha, it was only about 60,000,000. If the rule of reincarnation based on the Buddhist theory (Samusara; which all things are in flux through the endless circle of birth, death, and rebirth; the circle of transmigration) is the universal truth, the absolute value of the population should be fixed and not change eternally, because we repeat death and rebirth.

In the year 1,700 AD, which was 2,300 years after the Buddha's death, the number of human beings had reached 600,000,000 which was ten times more than in Buddha's era. Then Pandora's box was opened by the dropping of the atomic bomb on Hiroshima and Nagasaki in 1945, ending the Second World War. After that we experienced unprecedented population growth, and at the same time, science technology had advanced remarkably. The population explosion on the earth occurred as if human beings were cancer cells propagated abnormally in one stroke, from advanced cancer to terminal cancer, and the world population reached 5,670,000,000

Chapter Four ☆ The Conclusion

in 1995.

In 1995 the Islamic sphere developed the atomic bomb to use against the Christian sphere, which was just 50 years, a half century, after the dropping of the atomic bombs on Hiroshima and Nagasaki. The mass destruction weapons spread to the Christian sphere, the socialist sphere, the Hindu sphere, and the Islamic sphere, and caused an extremely delicate situation. So now, the danger of extinction of the earth has become reality.

In the year 2,000, the world population reached 6 billion, which was 1,000 times more than 6,000 years ago and 100 times more than the era of Buddha, and 10 times more than in 1,700, only 300 years ago. Since the terrestrial life entity had begun from a single cell of bacteria, it is amazing that the cells of human beings have increased up to 60 trillion, throughout 3.8 billion years. If we compared the earth to a life entity, when human beings, like the cancer cell of the terrestrial life, reached 5,670,000,000 people, it was exactly the time that the earth itself had fallen into a critical illness condition, like a terminal cancer patient. Because of the egoism of cancer cells, called human beings, all existing things began to collapse, such as the breakup of families, the destruction of the natural environment in the nature world, the social order, and the collapse of the global economic system, etc.

The threats of the nuclear bomb and the threats of cancer are extremely similar in that the same mechanism by which some kind of initiation factors in the microscopic world and the incidence of chain reaction, occurs. They are a dangerous and destructive system which directs the whole to total ruin when they reach "the critical of nuclear fission" by increasing the occurred threat disorderly.

When the nuclear fission of atoms, the "nuclear fission" of cells, and the "nuclear fission" of population become the real threat, it will be the macro threat to the entire earth which is, for instance, the outbursts of terrorist attacks with the mass destruction weapons, and the micro threat as the onset explosion of cancer.

To survive this termination era in religions, we should have the wisdom to convert radically from earth logical religious doctrines to the cosmological PARAREVO theory, direct the existing purpose and the existing value of life to truth, and suggest the path to the real spiritual evolution. Otherwise, there is no future for human beings and the earth. You might think we human beings are not so foolish, however this has been proven in history by the fact of religious wars. It would be absolutely impossible to complete spiritual evolution and graduate from the earth with the history of struggle by religious theory based on *the male theory of power, domination, struggle and destruction* which was advocated by male saints who were the relative objectivity. The definitive difference between the past struggle history and the future struggle history is whether or not there is a nuclear threat in the center of the struggle. So, there is no change in men's foolish theory at all.

The first year of the 21st century, from September 11, 2001, which was the beginning of the religious struggle, to September 11, 2010, the reviving period of 9 years, on the earth scale, was over. There were 3 steps of every 3 year period, which are 3 years reviving period, 3 years development period, and 3 years completion period. From September 11, 2010 to September 11, 2100, will be the end of the 90 years development period on the earth scale, with 3 steps of every 30 years reviving period, development period, and

Chapter Four ☆ The Conclusion

completion period. And the 900 years completion period will be over on September 11, 3000 which is from September 11, 2100, with 3 steps of every 300 years of reviving period, development period, and completion period.

As we can see from this, in order for all human beings to achieve spiritual evolution as homo cosmology, the cosmic life entity, all future histories for human beings are inserted to complete with "the cosmic number" of "3" by passing the historical journey of 3 steps of reviving period, development period, and completion period, with the circle of 3 years, 30 years and 300 years, by the completion number of 21 as 2001, 2010 and 2100. We are now in the journey of the development period of 90 years since September 11, 2010, and we human beings must evolve to the philosophical life entity, which is mature homo philosophical by September 11, 2100. To do that, we human beings must achieve evolution as homo philosophical by completing Self-Enlightenment and spiritual evolution by the rule of change by birth and re-birth with spiritually wise women, shift the direction from the male type sexual dominating structure within the undifferentiated sexual desire world based on the rule of "body is subjective and spirit is objective," to the female type love integrating structure within the highly differentiated sexual integrated world based on the rule of "spirit is subjective and body is objective." Otherwise, we will be not able to welcome the day of September 11, 2100, peacefully.

4-100. The PARAREVO theory is the thought of remorse

The thought of grudge is the rule of the earth. With this thought, we are directed to victim consciousness, and shift the responsibility to others, because we are dominated by physical desire and uncomfortable feelings, which were derived from the root of the instinctive survival consciousnesses based on the rule of "body is subjective and spirit is objective." With this thought of grudge, truth which is the relative subjectivity, is dominated by fact, the relative objectivity, according to the principle of dimensional domination by external separation, with the theory of good and evil and the theory of superiority or inferiority, making acquisition competition for others evaluation intense, falling into victim consciousness by saying that "that person is wrong," "it is this person's responsibility," or "that person is the problem," etc., repeating criticism and attacks, and directs to the shifting of responsibility, which is Self-escape for Self-defense.

The thought of remorse is the rule of the universe. With this thought, we are directed to the Self-responsibility principle which is to face all things with modesty and humility and accept everything with gratitude and happiness. We carry the sentiment of repentance and penitence because of the offender consciousness in the cosmic dimension with regret of one's own sinfulness and poor mind, which was derived from the root of SHINSEI and the spiritual consciousness entity based on "spirit is subjective and body is objective." With this thought of remorse, fact, which is the relative objectivity, is surpassed by truth, the relative subjectivity, according to the principle of dimensional integration by internal

Chapter Four ☆ The Conclusion

separation, free from the theory of good and evil and the theory of superiority and inferiority, and we make the best Self-effort in order to establish SHINSEI integration consciousness and accept all things unconditionally and totally with gratitude and happiness, by Self-responsibility based on the offender consciousness of the cosmic dimension.

This is because *the earth star is the prison planet* and when we perceive the earth from the infinite universe dimension, we are nothing but prisoners. So, *from the cosmic dimension, there are no victims on the earth, there are only offenders.* The way of thinking of the cosmic dimension and the earth dimension are directed totally opposite in the spiritual dimension, and there is huge difference between them. When people are in the lower dimension, they have stronger victim consciousness and shifting responsibility is the natural thing to do. The atonement theory of the cross of Jesus is the easier phenomenon to understand about the principle of dimensional domination by external separation based on the thought of grudge. Obviously, Jesus made *the conclusion of offender* toward outside when he said "Lord, please forgive them," based on the theory of grudge, in which he was the victim who was executed by faultless sin and they were the offenders to execute him.

There are no special things in the universe. However, we have created certain special things, such as Jesus and Buddha; by the same token, we also created discrimination and domination openly, on the earth. The fact that Jesus and Buddha existed on the earth wearing the physical body proves that they were nothing but prisoners as well. If there is a special or unusual being existing in the universe, discrimination would occur and *the principle of nonaggression and nonintervention* would be destroyed, and the rule of freedom itself would collapse.

In the rule of the universe, the principle of nonaggression and nonintervention is exercised strictly in order to guarantee the rule of freedom, so that the things in the higher level never intervene or meddle in the things in the lower level selfishly by ignoring this rule. So, *the universe will never take sides.*

In the rule of the earth, *since we consider particular persons as a special existence and treat them as special, we lose universality. As a result, deceitful gurus and dictators appear and continue to make the religious groups and the dictatorships of ugly pyramidal dominating structure.*

Jesus had just fallen into victim consciousness, according to the principle of dimensional domination by external separation based on the theory of good and evil, and abandoned the responsibility of assignment by shifting Self-responsibility to the Jewish and Roman soldiers. I feel he played a lifetime performance, immersed in the ultimate narcissist of Self-satisfaction and narcissism, and died by playing a tragic hero beautifully as his own work. After Jesus's death, by the intention of religious followers, they glorified the ultimate performance, put him up as the Messiah, and legalized the religious domination of dependent type of salvation, historically.

Since people who live the way of PARAREVO understand the spiritual world and prepare for the spiritual life, they never feel conflict, pain, or anguish in their daily life. They accept everything, unconditionally, according to Self-responsibility based on SHINSEI, so they never violate the separation borderline between themselves and others, like Jesus did. Since in the spiritual world, only the

Chapter Four ☆ The Conclusion

consciousness based on SHINSEI exists and becomes phenomenon and manifests, PARAREVO people understand uncomfortable feelings will create uncomfortable phenomena, and the feelings of gratitude and happiness will create the world of individual art based on free love.

People who live the PARAREVO way understand that unfortunate reality and tragic phenomena are all connoted in the consciousness of themselves as the cause, assignment, and problem, based on the thought of remorse. For example, when you carry the bad habits in your mind which you don't even easily realize by yourself, such as lying, harmful thoughts to others, or to steal something you want from others, etc., it might manifest the opposite way and similar phenomena would happen to you. If you are a victim of those phenomena, instead of blaming people who offended you, you should consider that the cause, problem, and assignment of this phenomenon exist inside of you. PARAREVO people will make the best Self-effort to direct to the thought of remorse by the view of cosmic dimension, according to dimensional integration by internal separation, based on the rule of "spirit is subjective and body is objective."

In order to complete Self-Enlightenment and spiritual evolution by directing the spiritual dimension to a higher level, from Homo sapiens (person of intelligence) to Homo philosophical (person of philosophy) and then to Homo cosmology (person of the universe), how to understand the fact and the method to guide your truth by the philosophy and the theory of spirit based on *the thought of remorse,* are clearly defined by the PARAREVO theory. The thought of remorse directs the arrow of the consciousness to yourself, and takes all things as the result of the fact reflected and phenomenalized by the truth of your cause, the assignment, and the problem connoted in yourself.

If unfair or unreasonable things happen to PARAREVO people, they understand that it is caused by them because the unfairness or unreasonableness inside of them was brought up as a phenomenon, so even though a fact made it seem like they were the victim, they accept it as the phenomenalized problem and assignment due to their carelessness, sinfulness, meanness and ugliness. Then they distinguish the "soul mind" and the "body mind," according to the principle of dimensional integration by internal separation, and direct the "soul mind," the relative subjectivity, to achieve Self-Enlightenment and spiritual evolution with SHINSEI integration consciousness by their best Self-effort, accept as they are unconditionally and totally with gratitude and happiness, based on the equation: *release one`s own ONSHU ("body mind"), by loving the ONSHU*.

The PARAREVO theory clarifies the responsibility toward the problem and the assignment in our life of offender and victim, and comprehends that victim has a greater responsibility toward the problem and the assignment than offender. It is because we tend to become violent by the victim consciousness. And when people with victim consciousness leave the earth, they go to the ugly spiritual world by keeping the poor ONSHU, become violent themselves, will return to the earth by re-descending according to the rule of reincarnation, and they will easily commit crimes, which are totally opposite from the things they experienced once before.

PARAREVO people do not live with the thought of grudge based on fact, but make the best Self-effort to live with the thought of remorse based on truth. It is because no fact in the universe exists over truth, and in the spiritual world, only truth exists and it is the world to be phenomenalized by truth.

4-101. Homo cosmology and "Regeneration of SHINSEI and soul"

Since the "atonement theory of Jesus on the cross," the Buddhist theory of retribution, and many religious theories which legalize polygamy are all religious doctrines of earth, and it's theoretical framework and value created by men with the theory of *power, domination, struggle and destruction* based on the principle of dependence and domination, it is an undeniable fact that they have developed the religious struggles all over the world. If we stubbornly follow the pyramidal dominating structure created by the religious theories of which man's founders and originators are in the center, in the era of the termination, human beings will certainly face the era of the destruction of the earth by nuclear threat, as a result of the struggles by the theoretical framework and values with the lack of a capacity to accept each other.

There is only one way to solve this problem. We should accept the cosmological theoretical framework and value, which integrates all religions, and complete paradigm revolution from the male type dominating structure to the female type integrating structure by spiritually wise women. Otherwise, there is no future for human beings or future for the earth. It is because the physical evolution and the spiritual evolution have been done for improvement of physical conditions and spiritual quality according to the spiritual dimension in each era, by *the rule of change by birth and re-birth in the womb, which is the sanctuary for evolution.* Children of Christianity, Islam, and Buddhism are all born through the body and the spirit and mind of their mother, but not born from religion.

Therefore, history will not change by the male supremacy, forever. However, if women become spiritually wise and convert history to the female supremacy, it is possible to change the history of 3.8 billion years, drastically, in only a few generations. In order to do so, we should understand the mechanism and the system of the birth of terrestrial life and the process of evolution, and clear the equation to evolve to a new spiritual dimension, and show the path we human beings must take.

In the infinite universe, the spiritual world (the intangible substantial world) and the material world (the tangible substantial world) form the harmony and order by the relative original power with the slight fluctuation of imperfection, however, there are malfunctions, and a phenomenon sometimes happens, like the giant impact when Mars collided with earth. When such phenomena happen, a big fluctuation occurs in space, so a big crack opens between the spiritual world and the material world, and the gap of *"the fuzzy region"* called the universe pocket appears, and then the path between the spiritual world and the material world opens.

When Mars collided with earth, a part of earth was stripped off and released to space, and formed the Moon. Water which existed on Mars at that time was all scattered in space from the impact and became blocks of ice. Those blocks of ice were gradually gathered by the gravitation of the moon, and were pulled to the earth by

Chapter Four ☆ The Conclusion

the stronger gravitation of the earth, so the mission and role of the fourth planet, Mars, was delegated to the third planet, Earth.

The order of the spiritual dimension in the solar system is determined by the binding force of the sun, so the farther out the ring of the planet is, the greater degree of freedom, and it becomes a granulated planet from materialized planet and furthermore, it will become a gaseous planet with the increase of the degree of freedom. The planet in the lowest spiritual dimension in the solar system is Mercury, and the next is Venus, and Earth is placed as the third planet in the lower spiritual dimension. Neptune is placed in the highest spiritual dimension in the solar system. The reason Venus is a symbol of Satan, called Lucifer, and the planet of ill fortune for earth, is because it is located in a lower spiritual dimension than earth. Through this process, the Earth became the planet to play the mission and the role of the prison star. On the earth, the relative structure with amino acid and DNA were formed, and when the preparation and the environment for life were done, the spiritual consciousness entity descended materially through the fuzzy region, the pocket of the universe, based on the relative wave in the spiritual dimension and the rule of the relative original power, and a bacteria as a primitive life entity was born.

The bacteria and virus were extremely simple "sex unified life entity" without sexual differentiation. The mechanism for spiritual evolution is led to the sexual desire consciousness, which directs the life chain and the preservation of species, and gradually being directed to the sexual differentiation by the intention to seek the stronger stimulus of love and happiness, and at the same time, physical evolution was done. Anthropoid apes such as orangutans, gorillas and chimpanzees created pyramidal dominating structure by forming a pecking order by sexual relationship with a boss at the center and conduct sexual relationships frequently, regardless of male or female, and regardless of whether or not it is a breeding season. That is the difference between anthropoid apes and other animals.

The origin of modern humans descended from the woman called "Mitochondrial Eve," in Africa about 160,000 years ago, and agriculture started in different regions of the world all at once 6,000 years ago, and at the same time, civilization occurred and the foundation of modern humans was created. Seeing this fact, the contents in the Old Testament, 6,000 years ago, might be consistent with human embryology.

When Homo sapiens achieved spiritual evolution, it was the time humans started to wear clothes. *The release and freeing from undifferentiated sexual desire consciousness* is the driving force for spiritual evolution. As written in "Paradise Lost" in the Old Testament, Adam and Eve had no shame being naked; however, Eve first freed herself from sexual disgrace and disorder and covered the lower part (genitals) with a fig leaf, and Adam followed. I think this meant that they began to grow the sexual separation consciousness, being directed to the sexual order and achieved spiritual evolution to Homo sapiens as new dimension.

However, the religious theory by the male type sexual domination interprets totally opposite. It was interpreted as the original sin which was breaking the commandments of God.

Now the serpent was more crafty than any of the wild animals

Chapter Four ☆ The Conclusion

the Lord God had made. He said to the woman, "Did God really say, 'You must not eat from any tree in the garden'?"

The woman said to the serpent, "We may eat fruit from the trees in the garden, but God did say, 'You must not eat fruit from the tree that is in the middle of the garden, and you must not touch it, or you will die.' " You will not certainly die," the serpent said to the woman. "For God knows that when you eat from it your eyes will be opened, and you will be like God, knowing good and evil."

When the woman saw that the fruit of the tree was good for food and pleasing to the eye, and also desirable for gaining wisdom, she took some and ate it. She also gave some to her husband, who was with her, and he ate it. Then the eyes of both of them were opened, and they realized they were naked; so they sewed fig leaves together and made coverings for themselves. (Genesis 3.1~3.7)

If the act of breaking the commandments of God was the Fall of Man and the original sin, human beings still might conduct chaotic sexual relationships and be naked by undifferentiated sexual desire consciousness, just like chimpanzee bonobos. Eve did not hide her lower part by fig leaves because of the sin consciousness against the sexual depravity and breaking God`s commandments. She desired to direct the sexual order by the sexual classification, and by wearing clothes, the woman made the protection from sexual depravity, so that the woman and the man began to be separated as "sex separation life entities." Since at the moment when the primitive life entity was born on the earth star, life had connoted the two major desire consciousnesses called the dietary desire consciousness and the sexual desire consciousness, which were the instinctive survival consciousnesses as a fate, if the concept of depravity exists, we had already been depraved from that moment.

The interpretation of the original sin by the religious theory of male subjectivity and the interpretation of spiritual evolution by the PARAREVO theory of female subjectivity are totally opposite. Even though what God and serpent insisted regarding justice to being naked and injustice to dress in clothing, the interpretation and validation toward the sexual ethics in the process of spiritual evolution are absolutely different. The fruit of the tree centered in the garden indicates SHINSEI connoted inside oneself. So, "do not eat and do not touch the fruit" means to not embrace or provoke SHINSEI, and it was clearly meant to interrupt the path to spiritual evolution and eternal life by the principle of dimensional integration.

It also means that *the higher level of dimensional sexual differentiation is the important mechanism and the equation to achieve spiritual evolution to higher human beings.* As I have mentioned many times, the equation for physical evolution and spiritual evolution are led to women, the relative subjectivity. According to the principle of dimensional integration based on the theory of love, integration, harmony and creation of women, physical evolution and spiritual evolution will be completed in *the womb which is the sanctuary for evolution,* based on the rule of change by birth and re-birth.

The spiritual dimension of women will determine physical evolution and spiritual evolution, and the important factor to determine the spiritual dimension is whether the woman connotes *undifferentiated sexual desire consciousness* more, or whether she has achieved the *higher differentiated sexual integration consciousness* by her spiritual evolution. There will be a huge

Chapter Four ☆ The Conclusion

difference in the spiritual dimension of a fetus if the mother's soul is in the lower spiritual dimension and conceived her child by *lewd sexual relationship* or if she is in a higher spiritual dimension and conceived her child by her motivation to receive a soul from a higher dimension, *"sacred conception relationship."*

It is because the spiritual evolution and the physical evolution of a fetus are completed as a substantial work in the mother's womb by the rule of change by birth and re-birth. It is also a preparation for important spiritual work to complete *the equation of regeneration of SHINSEI and soul,* when we are going to the spiritual world of the universe. Based on the rule of "spirit is subjective and body is objective," physical evolution is done by genetic regeneration, according to the individuality of the soul of the fetus, and spiritual evolution will be completed by the relative original power based on the mind and spirit of the mother and the soul of the fetus, by directing the spiritual consciousness entity of the fetus to the higher level by the principle of dimensional integration by maternal love.

Once you are born to this world, you must build the love pair system with "sexually pure women" and "sexually pure men," who are clearly differentiated sexually by SHINSEI unity, according to the true existing purpose and the existing value of their life, and go up the spiritual dimension based on the mind and spirit, and sublimate the six steps from love in the individual dimension to the family dimension, to clan dimension, to the ethnic group dimension, to the national dimension, to the love of the earth dimension, based on the way of life of PARAREVO which is explained as follows. We draw the separation borderline between now and past/future, and between "I" and others, establish Self-integrity, and accept everything as it is unconditionally and totally with gratitude and happiness, and direct ourselves to universal Self-creation which manifests the individual art based on free love, eternally, by SHINSEI integration consciousness, and by doing so we are able to raise the degree of freedom of love and the degree of consciousness.

"A sexually pure man and woman" are the pair system of Logos, who can face each other according to love based on the rules and principles of the universe. An ordinary couple has a relationship by the physical desire of egoism and narcissism according to non-rational sexual desire based on the rules and principles of the earth. Thus, it is important that the relationship of man and woman is either a sustainable platonic love of Logos, or one with momentary pleasure by non-sustainable egoism and narcissism of Eros.

A sexually pure woman united with the sun (the feminine) and a sexually pure man united with the moon (the masculine) must form the pair system of sun /moon integration consciousness, spiritually. Without this process of forming the love pair system of SHINSEI unity, we are not able to go to the path as a life entity in the galaxy spiritual dimension beyond the solar system.

If we replace the relationship between woman and man on the earth to the one in the universe, the sun is a woman and the moon is a man. The sun is the light and the moon can shine by the light of the sun. Thus, the more woman accomplishes the spiritual evolution, the more man can accomplish the spiritual evolution by the change by birth and re-birth as well.

The existence of the sun and the moon give us the closest feeling of the universe from the earth which we can actually realize, and their meaning is very important to us. We must convert from the undifferentiated sexual desire world of the male type sexual dominating structure to the highly differentiated sexual integrated world of the female type love integrating structure; create the highly-differentiated sexual integration consciousness with sexually pure women, as the sexual subject, and sexually pure men as the sexual object. And then, we can achieve Self-Enlightenment and spiritual evolution to the philosophical life entity, Homo philosophical, from the intellectual life entity, Homo sapiens, by establishing the sexual ethics which distinguish the higher life.

When you accomplish the role and the responsibility in this life, and go to the spiritual world on the extension idea of preparation for the spiritual life, by the rule of change by birth and re-birth based on *the equation of the regeneration of true soul (the free spiritual consciousness entity according to the love and independence of universe),* the key (spiritual penis) of a sexually pure man coincides with the key way (spiritual vagina) of a sexually pure woman and match exactly, the door of the womb, which is the sanctuary for the spiritual love of woman, opens and receives the soul of a man unconditionally. It becomes *the sex integrated life entity,* to re-birth the soul of the man to *SHINSEI integrated life entity* by the sexual integration consciousness of the woman, and make the man's soul conceiving it to the spiritual world in the new higher spiritual dimension. By doing so, the spiritual consciousness entity of the woman will be re-birthed to SHINSEI integrated life entity synchronically and simultaneously, and will complete the spiritual evolution as Homo cosmology which is the cosmological life entity completely freed from the physical body.

With that mechanism, which makes the birth of the universal

relative original power sustainable by the relative structure of the slight fluctuation of imperfection, SHINSEI and the spiritual consciousness entity are directed to the higher level according to the principle of dimensional integration, and they prepare the system which becomes possible to exist eternally, and then complete themselves as Homo cosmology. Homo cosmology combines both the mechanism and the system, and it is called *SHINSEI integrated life entity based on the integrated type of the Mobius loop, which is the Mobius system that men, the object, is integrated to women, the subject, neutrally and moderately in a slight fluctuation, and form harmony and order. The Mobius loop expresses infinity and eternity.*

As you can see from this explanation, women and men who are even very excellent and distinguished persons, such as saints, are not able to complete love by themselves, alone. Since the subject of love is women, and only women are given the spiritual function for the physical release and spiritual evolution, without changing the soul of men by birth, women's soul would never be re-birthed. Based on the rule of entropy relativity, *the right of approval in this world is controlled by men, however, in the spiritual world, the right of approval is all in complete control of women.* If we do not follow this equation, nobody can graduate from the earth star, and unless we transcend the seventh borderline of the spiritual evolution, we will re-descend to this world over and over according to the rule of reincarnation.

For we human beings, through the life evolution, the process to become the cosmic life entity, is to start from "the sex unified life entity" called bacteria, the primitive life entity, to go through the middle differentiated sexual separation consciousness from undifferentiated sexual desire consciousness, to accomplish evolution to "the sex separation life entity" which is comprehended to the highly differentiated sex integration consciousness that considers women as the sexual subject and men as the sexual object, to become "the sex integrated life entity" according to the equation of regeneration of SHINSEI and soul in the spiritual world, and to complete Homo cosmology as "SHINSEI integrated life entity" by the rule of spiritual change by birth and re-birth, and it is possible to reach the spiritual dimension as the cosmic life entity.

Spiritually wise men understand that women are the relative subjectivity and men are the relative objectivity, so they do not have contempt for or look down on women, instead they face, sincerely, to the spiritual intelligence and spiritual sense of spiritually wise women, and can direct Self-Enlightenment and spiritual evolution by assisting women with modesty and humility. Men do not go to the path of the spiritual evolution as long as they are re-birthed by women. The pattern of thinking of men is directed to the physical desire, the "body mind." The pattern of mentality of women is directed to the mind and spirit, the "soul mind." Women have been fed up with the men's domination with their motivation of this physical sexual desire. Men must make Self-effort to release this ONSHU of women. It is because the equation of Self-Enlightenment and spiritual evolution for them exists only there. "Spiritually wise women" are the ones who hold the casting board for the future of human beings and the earth.

If you have chosen to be a woman in this life, you have ONSHU as a woman who was a sex slave of men in a past life and had surrendered to the power and domination by men. So, releasing this ONSHU will be the important key for the spiritual evolution. The sex relationship should be very noble, however, because of the lack of love, it has become impure and indecent because of physical desire. The reality is, ONSHU of women toward sex is too strong. This ONSHU forms the victim consciousness of women. Because of it, women could not stand as the subject of love even if they were supposed to, and that, I feel, is the root of all problems on the earth. It is so important how much women can integrate hatred toward sex by Self-effort with forgiveness and tolerance. Women cannot re-birth men or be re-birthed themselves by having ONSHU toward sex.

Since there is only cause and effect in the universe, actually there is no victim and offender on the earth, either. The cause and effect begins with me and ends with me. The reality of the effect called sex discrimination is by the cause called me. Feminism and the appeal of equal rights for both sexes would not solve the issue. There would not be any future for the earth, unless women give up the habit of being the victim of sex, and unite the earth with their internal energy of love, creation, harmony and integration.

The cosmic bible is the guidebook to graduate from the earth star, which is the prison planet, and shows the path that human beings should follow from now on, by directing us to the truth of undeniable existentialism, and let us walk that path by the principle of Self-responsibility of each person. All things are led to the truth of Self-management by Self-determination and Self-completion by Self-responsibility, based on the rule of freedom. It is up to you to decide whether you evolve to Homo cosmology, which is the life entity of the infinite universe, or whether you remain as Homo sapiens, which is the life entity on the earth star, the prison planet.

The Equation of Spiritual Evolution

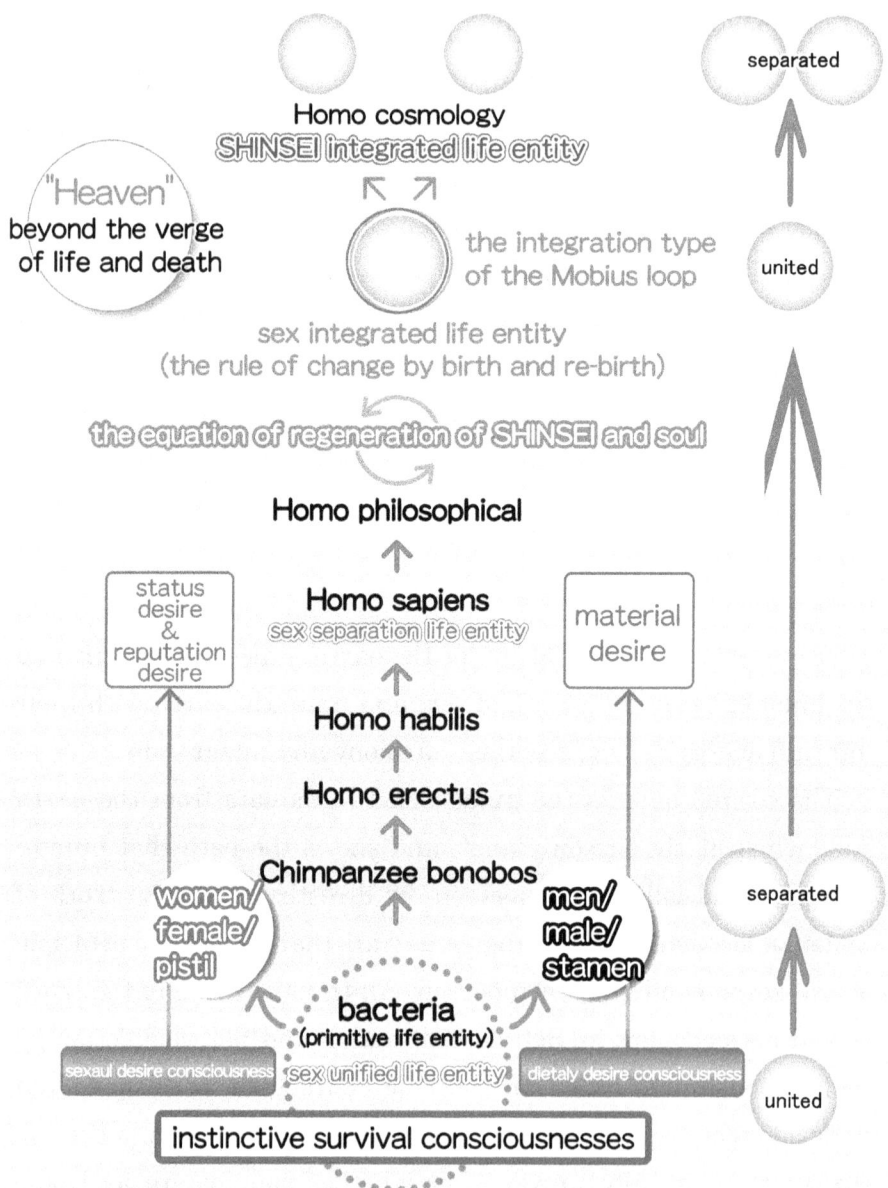

For more information please contact us :
Self-Healing Study and Practice Group
(info@selfhealing.co.in)

www.ingramcontent.com/pod-product-compliance
Lightning Source LLC
Chambersburg PA
CBHW060115170426
43198CB00010B/903